Living Without
Your Twin

[handwritten inscription]

Dear Carlene
I look forward
to hearing from you —
God bless
Betty Jean Case

Living Without
Your Twin

Betty Jean Case

Tibbutt Publishing
Portland, Oregon

Cataloging in Publication Data
Case, Betty Jean
   Living Without Your Twin/Betty Jean Case. –
Portland, OR: Tibbutt Pub. Co., © 1993.
   p. , cm.
   Parts of work originally published in: We are twins,
but who am I? © 1991.
   ISBN: 0-9629948-1-2

1. Twins–Psychology. 2. Twins–Death.
3. Bereavement. 4. Alienation (Social psychology)
I. Title.

BF723.T9   155.4'44 dc20
    Library of Congress Card Number 93-61030

About the Author

Betty Jean Case has a fraternal twin sister, fraternal twin brothers and is the grandmother of fraternal twin boys. Having grown up in a totally twin environment she never gave thought to the effects twinship might have had upon her life until she saw her grandsons being compared as infants. It was then that she began to reflect back upon her life as a twin and pondered the question, "What effect has twinship had upon my life?" In going to the library in search of better understanding of the twin relationship she found nothing that would better help her learn the thoughts of twins. Determined to find out how twins felt about being twins, she created a five page questionnaire for twins – exploring in depth three main areas: Childhood of twin, parent/child relationship and the adult relationship. With questionnaire in hand she went to over 800 identical and fraternal twins, basically from the ages of 20-70, a fifty year span, asking these twins to reflect back upon their life lived as a twin. Her first book, *We Are Twins, But Who Am I?*, lets you know what she learned. Many twins had never given thought to their own twinship and she was thanked for giving them a vehicle through which they could express feelings that had never been shared, or never really known before.

Since Betty Jean has all of her twin siblings living she did not address the issue of twin loss until she received several hundred responses from twins. It was then that she realized the need for further research in the area of twin loss. This book is the result of greater exploration into the feelings of twins who have lost their twin through death, estrangement, murder and suicide. In her first book she devoted one chapter to Twin Loss but in this, her latest book, she has done further research into the area of estrangement of twins, suicide and murder of one twin.

This is a book that gives twins who have known such loss a chance to express their feelings and lets the reader know how these surviving twins have coped with such a loss. Suggestions for healing are given.

It is Betty Jean's wish that any of you who would like to be in contact with her is most welcomed and encouraged to write to her. She will make every effort to put you in touch with another person who might possibly make the healing process a smoother one.

You may contact her by writing:
Betty Jean Case
Tibbutt Publishing
0438 SW Palatine Hill Road
Portland, Oregon 97219
Telephone (503) 246-6748

Acknowledgments

I am greatly indebted to the twinless twins who have searched their souls and been willing to share their thoughts–and their pain, with you. They have done so in hopes that by their sharing, your journey may be made with greater ease.

It is impossible to name all of the people who have played a part in making this book a reality. A spoken word, an approving look, a suggestion offered at the right time all contributed to the book's completion.

I must say thank you to my three little granddaughters, Alexandra, Jocelyn and Johnna for keeping me young at heart. And to my supportive husband, Laurel, who has always encouraged me to try my own wings.

My sincere thanks goes to Terri Walker who has been side by side with me as we worked to make this book not only informative but interesting, helpful and comforting.

Many thanks to Bob Keene for indexing and to my son Bob Case for editorial assistance.

This book is lovingly dedicated to Dr. Raymond W. Brandt, and in memory of his twin brother, Robert, for his immeasurable contribution in behalf of twinless twins everywhere.

Foreword

Twins have always held the general public in a spell of fascination and curiosity; however often the public's knowledge and awareness ends at those levels. For those who are privileged to count twins among their family, relatives or friends, there are dimensions of uncanny communication – links as strong as steel. The unique bond of twinship dates from conception and when it is torn in half through death, profound repercussions can be expected.

Betty Jean Case introduced this subject in her first book, *We Are Twins, But Who Am I?* with an entire chapter on the loss of a twin. She further explores this under-recognized subject in the following pages, offering insights into different kinds of loss, occurring at various stages through the lifecycle. Few will remain dry-eyed after reading of the anguish and abandonment experienced when a twin is lost through estrangement, adoption, murder, illness or an accident.

Many times, people erroneously assume that when a twin is lost, "at least the other one is left". This is no consolation to the parents or family as one individual can never replace another. In fact, because of the dualism involved it is a most severe form of loss; the presence of "one-half" is a persistent reminder that accentuates the loss of the other. When an adult twin dies, the myriad silken threads of twinship may be submerged by family and friends supporting the parents while unintentionally overlooking the twin. If this tragedy happens around the time of birth, parents have the polemic task of grieving the loss of one twin, while needing to bond with the survivor.

Twins, especially monozygotic (identical) ones, enjoy a bond even closer than the symbiotic connection between mother and child. Cell by cell, their earliest growth and development takes place within a shared oceanic world. Italian psychoanalyst Alessandra Piontelli has spent hours using ultrasound as a "window on the womb". Her intriguing observations indicate just how early the twin interaction begins. Furthermore, the individual personality traits of each twin, together with aspects of their social life as a couple are carried on with amazing similarity and continuity after birth. It is no surprise then, when we read of adults in this book who, for the first time in middle life, suddenly flash back to a perinatal loss of a twin and are flooded with grief. This pre- and perinatal period of loss of a multiple has been the focus on my own personal and professional experiences. As many more twins "vanish" during pregnancy than will ever be known, we can estimate that a considerable number of adults are unaware twin survivors. These are frequently individuals who have an intense interest in twins without any obvious personal reason, such as multiples in the family.

To be human is to be in danger. Surviving twins, as one expressed it to me, "perhaps have a closer connection with the divine" through this very special fate. We can all learn more from twins with respect to the possibilities of human "knowing" – dimensions of contact that do not fit into our understanding of the physical world and concrete knowledge. In particular, we can learn from *Living Without Your Twin* how important it is to honor the extraordinary potential of twinship – long and strong – before death tears them asunder.

A twin is a gift, a privilege, a partner for life. Consequently, it is necessary to ensure that the twinship is not buried with the twin. Betty Jean Case has provided a wonderful service in exploring this painful topic. Survivors, and their friends and family, will appreciate the grounded advice she offers for coping with the solo journey that follows when one must live on without the other.

Elizabeth Noble

Elizabeth Noble is the author of seven books and the founder of the Obstetrics and Gynecology Section of the American Physical Therapy Association. She wrote the first edition of the "bible", Having Twins: A Parent's Guide to Pregnancy, Birth and Early Childhood, *years before she concluded through her personal regression work that she was the survivor of a first-trimester twin loss. She subsequently added an extensive chapter on the loss of a multiple in the second edition of that book. In her 1993 book,* Primal Connections: How Our Experiences From Conception through Birth Influence our Emotions, Behavior and Health, *she describes survivors of pre- and perinatal loss of a multiple, how they relived the experience and how it affected their lives. Elizabeth Noble lives on Cape Cod with her family and is the director of Women's Health Resources in Harwich, MA. She is on the advisory board of the Center for Loss in Multiple Birth (CLIMB) and gives lectures and workshops across the U.S. and abroad on issues of pre-and perinatal health.*

Introduction

Turning 'we' to 'I' is not easy for a twin. It is inevitable that a twin will have to learn to separate and establish their own identity as they mature, but that natural process can be complicated by external circumstances. Emotional estrangement can bring anguish, guilt, loneliness and confusion as each twin tries to sort out their feelings and their understanding of themselves and their twin. When a twin loses their twin to death it is a long process, and a painful one as they work toward thinking of themselves as one person instead of two.

The intensity of loss a twin feels on losing a twin will depend on their previous closeness. It is important for family and friends to recognize the intensity of the bond that exists between twins.

Identical twins often feel as 'one'. These are twins who may feel each other's pain, share each other's thoughts, and feel incomplete when they are apart. These twins are reminded of their twin every time they look into a mirror. More than one twin wrote me of feeling quite embarrassed when the twin they waved at turned out to be their own reflection in a mirror. After losing their twin, surely these twins would have pangs of loss when they saw themselves again in a store mirror.

Fraternal twins are no more genetically alike than any other sibling. None of them told me that they felt they were half of a whole, as did a great number of identicals. Such comments as "She is me outside of me," as some identicals wrote, were not said by fraternals.

This is not to say that fraternal twins do not feel an intense bond between them—many of them do—but the intense feelings that identicals shared with me convinces me that the genetic influence plays a great part in the reaction that twins have when they lose their twin.

The grieving process may take longer for some twins. Each person expresses their feelings in their own time and in a different way. Friends' and relatives' patience and understanding is very important in the grieving process.

Contents

1

Twin Loss Through Estrangement

TO HAVE A TWIN who is still living, and yet not to have them is a pain that some twins must endure. Twin estrangement can result from many situations. One reason may be jealousy of the twin's spouse. This is why it is so important that anyone who marries a twin know, long before the knot is tied, the relationship that exists between the twins. The repeating of marriage vows will never alter the feelings that twins have for one another. Their lives have been bonded forever and most often will remain that way as long as they live.

There are various degrees of estrangement. Extreme estrangement can result in a twin never having contact with their twin for a number of years, sometimes never. Mild estrangement with a twin can be felt when they feel that they are no longer able to communicate with their twin on a feeling level, nor comfortable in sharing confidences with their twin.

It is most often the identical twin who has to deal

with estrangement. These twins are most likely to live parallel lives and feel the greatest degree of dependence upon one another. When a twin marries, it is often very hard for them to let go of their twin and transfer their loyalty to their spouse. Yet it is important that they be alert to signs of jealousy from their mate. Anyone who marries a twin will be smart to remember that a non-twin has never known the tight bond that can exist between some twins. The marriage vows ask that they transfer their loyalty to the one they are marrying, and that is not an easy task for a twin. My research shows that it is jealousy that most often causes twins to be estranged from one another.

Communication is a vital ingredient in nipping such feelings before they become a hard hurdle to jump. Twins should anticipate a certain amount of competition in the transition and give their twin time and emotional space to bond with their spouse.

Jackie and Judy, two very identical twins who have maintained a very healthy relationship in their marriages feel that communication is the key to success. What Judy and her husband had to say about being married to a twin is so good that I'd like to have you hear what he had to say as it so directly tells the feelings that make for healthy and happy twin marriages. In response to the question "How is it being married to a twin?" His main response was, "I got the best one." He thinks I am the best looking, most talented and have a better personality than Jackie does. Larry thinks the same thing about Judy. Jackie and I know they are both right. I'm sure our husbands didn't know what they were getting into. They didn't know they were marrying both of us, but fortunately we are all good friends and get along beautifully. Our husbands are friends, our daughters are friends and of course Jackie and I are twins.

In my book, *We Are Twins, But Who Am I?* I talk in the marriage chapter about a woman in her fifties who attends the Twinless Twins Support Group meeting at the International Twins Convention. Even though her twin is still living, she feels as though her twin is dead since she is denied being with her. Her husband is unreasonably jealous because of the closeness of the two. "It's just like having two husbands," one woman told me after she married her husband, who is an identical twin. She expressed delight that there was another who looked just like her husband.

What is it that causes twins to become estranged from one another? I am convinced that by far the majority of twins who find themselves unable to communicate with their twin or be with their twin on a friendly basis experience a torment that is hard to bear. May I suggest some of the reasons why some twins become estranged from their twin.

1. Lack of communication and real sharing of feelings is probably the number one reason twins feel separation from their twin.

2. Lack of understanding by the party involved in the twin relationship is another reason why a twin may become distanced from their twin. Some people who marry a twin are unaware of the almost exclusive relationship some twins have with one another. A spouse who is jealous of the time their mate spends with a twin may feel robbed and may deliver an either/or ultimatum.

3. Some twins do not operate on the same wavelength. Fraternal twins especially may be almost totally different in almost all ways and in extremely rare cases, one may be so unlike their twin in temperament and in mindset that they feel little desire for association.

3

I stress again this happens in very few twin relationships but it does happen. Following is an example of a set of twins being estranged for many years. This identical twin wrote, "I was the passive, dependent twin all my life. I left my twin for twenty years. I became strong assertive and independent. I saw my sister very rarely. I felt she robbed me of my personality. I hated my life because she gained control over me. I couldn't even commit suicide because of the pain I would cause her. I knew that it would virtually kill her. I am strong now and we have worked it out. I know she will never control me again."

4. The home environment certainly plays a big part in how twins are going to relate and feel about one another. I hasten here to add that parents of twins who find that their twin children want little to do with one another should not lay a guilt trip on themselves. But parents of twins do need to be aware of the damage that can be done when extreme favoritism results in one twin feeling less favored or when one twin is always the "winner", and the other twin the "loser".

Another twin, Carolyn Fine, wrote during a time of estrangement from her sister: "I have read and reread the chapter on "Loss of a Twin" in your book *We Are Twins, But Who Am I?* From it I get a glimmer of light as to what my life might be, without my twin around. I am overcome with bouts of despair. In my wildest dreams or nightmares, I cannot fathom what my life would be alone as one person. Twins are interwoven into a pattern like a piece of material-should a piece of this pattern be torn, it would be nothing but a torn, ravelled hole that cannot be mended again. A pattern undone and useless. Like a jigsaw puzzle with a piece missing. A picture never completed.

"I guess you could say that I am now going through a 'living sort of death' with my twin. Circumstances beyond our control have separated us. Death without the dying. It hurts like hell. I look at my twin covered in sadness. She is existing at living. No zest, no goals, nothing. I, on the other hand, am knocking myself out to grab hold of whatever happiness I can find. I am left undone. Hanging in limbo without her to share as we once did.

"I wonder, 'Did we die? Or are we living?' So again I open the book to the chapter that deals with 'The Loss of a Twin.' And I cry all alone. I cry and I wonder. When will I stop crying my silent tears?"

After this was written, Carolyn Fine's twin sister went through heart surgery. Carolyn and her brother-in-law found a new understanding during this ordeal. It is unfortunate that it may take the hint of death before a joining of minds comes about.

A history of abuse or incest will create communication problems in any family, and twins may find the estrangement particularly difficult. Ann, an identical twin woman, is estranged from her twin. After revealing that they had been victims of childhood incest, she writes:

"My memories of early childhood are quite pleasant. When we were in third or fourth grade, however, our lives changed. Our parents started to look at us differently. They would comment on 'how pretty Meg is,' but 'Ann does not hold her shoulders up' and 'walks funny.' They would also remark 'how smart Ann is'. I remember feeling very hurt about this. In my concrete child's mind, I got the message that Meg is prettier than me so she must be better than me. I began to withdraw and became very shy. Whenever anyone spoke to us,

Meg was quick to answer and I remained silent. It became common knowledge to everyone in our town that Meg spoke for both of us and was the more dominant twin. I felt this was okay, since Meg knew better than I about what to say and how to act. This continued throughout the rest of our childhood. The rest of my childhood and adolescence was spent as a shy, passive 'shadow' of my sister."

Through years of striving both for their own identity and for closeness, Ann describes suffering from grief, low self-esteem and depression. Her sister Meg initiated a dialogue between the twins about the childhood incest, after she had sought her own counseling and support. Ann also found insights and counseling, and began to heal. When her sister took the initiative to confront the family about the childhood incest of both twins, Ann felt hurt. "I felt she was still talking for both of us as she had done in our childhood. I also learned later that the family felt I had helped write the letter during our last visit together."

The more dominant twin felt her sister was being disloyal for not confronting the family in the same way. She decided to cut off the relationship with her sister.

"I am presently examining my relationship with my twin and what effect my twinning and the superimposed incest has had on my life as well as my sister's. The sad result is that we are estranged with many complex issues keeping us apart-issues of betrayal, victimization, dependency, competition, jealousy, and identity. I think that I am finally, at 40 years of age, asking the right questions. I am hopeful that with support and faith, I will receive the right answers, although I feel it is probably too late for my sister and me."

No twin should give up on the possibility of

reconciliation. Each twin has to accept the other as a unique person with their own thoughts and experiences. It is sad that this twin, as she evaluates the relationship at this time has concluded that: "My feeling now is that I wish my twin sister and I had been raised separately. Maybe then we could have been close friends as adults. I feel a great sadness that Meg and I have not cherished our 'twinness' enough to work through all of the difficult issues and find each other again, like we were as children...delighted with each other and proud to have a twin.

"I hope other twins who have problems with their relationship will seek help before it is too late."

The likelihood of a distinct parting of the ways of boy/girls twins is certainly a possibility when they can be so very different in many ways. The temperament of each child will greatly determine how they will each handle the remarks, the comparisons and the expectations that are placed upon them since they were born together. Parents of twins cannot start too early in working to learn the genetic make-up of each child and to build on the God-given strengths of each. It is imperative that parents be alert to the effect of each child upon the other. Much as parents would like to see each child gain from the strengths of the other and find them supporting each other, this is not often realistic.

If parents observe extreme dominance of one twin over the other, and see the one who is being dominated become meek and subservient to their twin, it is crucial that they take steps to change the pattern of behavior. It is not only important because of what it is doing to the one who is being put-down, but also because of what it is doing to the one who is learning to feel continued control of others.

7

Lillian Baker in her excellent book titled *A Book of Alms*, (1964 Copyright), "Reflections No. 1," is most expressive as she reflects back upon her life lived as a child and as a twin. She wrote, "Most of my childhood has been willfully blanked out or rejected. Many childhood reactions and naivete were experienced after I was already out of high school and on my own. How naive and immature I was! What childish bitterness and determination! How unprepared I was for the deep water when I had hardly been able to wade in by myself unaccompanied by my twin! And with so little foundation of faith and love to act as a buoy at high tide!"

Lillian Baker was estranged from her twin brother after a childhood filled with complex interactions. She describes her family as having a constant clashing of minds and personalities. She wrote:

"It is only be reflecting back in maturity that one can evaluate certain incidents and happenings, causes and effects, without the issue becoming clouded by prejudice and childish emotions. And because of my maturity I have such a different outlook and understanding of my childhood and my twinhood...for I was a twin, and being a twin affected my childhood considerably. Maybe the effect would not have been as considerable if we had been identical twins in any respect, that is if we were of the same sex or degree of intelligence or similar in personality or nature. No twins born could have been so opposite and yet so devoted. I won't use the term 'love' because I don't want to be one-sided about that issue. My brother was and always will be a cynic and even today I think he would be offended by the use of the sentimental term of 'love'. So I will settle for the term 'affectionate' because in very devious ways and always

8

trying to cover up any obvious display of such emotion, my twin gave me just enough affection at the right psychological moment for me to want nothing more than to live in his esteem and for him to be my sovereign. I, so unlike him, could not be an entity within myself."

It may sound preposterous, but we never quarrelled in childhood! Now I realize it was because I was too meek, afraid if I did not agree, my replies would sound ignorant...afraid he would use words that I did not understand then, and therefore had to be accepted as the truth, for I (like so many others) was too prone to accept that which I did not understand as the truth. Besides, I felt so completely rejected and outside my own family circle, I could not bear the thought of jeopardizing my position of jester in the 'king's' court, for I can remember happily now that the one thing I *was* able to do was to bring enough wit to dull the sharpness of his sarcasm. That was my usual way of apologizing for him to family or friends when his acid tongue hit its mark. I never felt the effects of his biting personally, but because I react emotionally to the feelings of others, I suffered with them but could not join them in what I knew would be a useless argument. He inevitably was the winner and in most cases he was strong enough in victory to bring the captives along with him for another ride to the next dispute. People could not help but admire his capacity for learning and his oratory ability. Shortly after we entered elementary school, he left me behind scholastically and finally graduated a full year ahead of me as valedictorian of his class.

"My twin and I have both matured each in our own way. We lead completely different lives with a different sense of values and still share no common philosophy or faith. At long last I have a separate identity, and I think

9

now he really loves me and respects me more for it.
(Maybe in truth I was the burden to him.) Yes, I think
somehow he has finally learned to love me, too. And
mature love is, after all, the most fulfilling."

2

Twin Loss Through Adoption

"I HAVE TO TELL YOU SOMETHING."
These are the words a next door neighbor said
to Barbara Parker, a thirty six year old woman
who had long known that she was adopted. Then the
neighbor broke the news, saying that her twin was next
door!

It all came as such a shock to her that at first it was
easier to believe that her neighbor had only found
someone who looked extremely like her. Barbara found
herself in a state of shock, and when she faced Ann
Blandon she said to her "How do I know you're my
sister?"

The mother of these twins had agreed to give up her
child, but didn't realize she was carrying twins. Barbara,
the first to be born was given to the couple awaiting her
birth. The doctor who delivered the two decided to adopt
Ann.

Unlike her sister, Ann Blandon had learned when
she was fifteen that she had been adopted and did have a

11

twin sister but had not started to search for her until the early 1980s.

There are many twins who now know the joy of twinship due to the diligent and painstaking efforts of two men, John Stroud, of England, and Professor Thomas Bouchard, of the University of Minnesota. Because of their work, they have been brought together and have been part of the ongoing study by the Minnesota Center for Twin and Adoption Research on the University Campus in Minneapolis/Saint Paul. Dr. Bouchard began this important research in 1979.

John Stroud's interest in re-uniting twins began when he counseled adopted children who were searching for their real parents. The war years caused much of the separation. It was when he came across several twins who were desperately trying to locate their twin that he felt a burning desire to aid in their finding one another.

Dr. Bouchard says that meeting John Stroud was a "godsend". All of the twins re-united by Stroud have visited Dr. Bouchard at the University of Minnesota. During my research for my first book *We Are Twins, But Who Am I?* I asked over 800 twin participants to respond to this question "As you look back over your life as a twin, is there any aspect of it you would change?" I share with you the comments made by an identical twin who was adopted along with her twin sister. She wrote, "Being an adoptee has had an extremely negative effect on my life. Because of that negativism I don't enjoy life. I am totally against adoptions unless all records are open and totally in favor of abortions. I would never wish my adoptive experience on anyone and supposedly we had a "good" adoption. Therefore if I could change one thing, I wish our birth mother had had an abortion if she chose not to keep us."

Another of my respondents who has not had a healthy relationship with her twin growing up, now as an adult says she sometimes wishes that she had not met her twin until they were grown women. She thinks that as adults they could have been friends. Perhaps it is the expectations to be alike and the competition that many twin experience with one another during their formative years that are the ingredients that make some twins feel the way this woman felt.

One of the other twin sets I interviewed spoke of the terrific support they gave one another when they were taken to the children's home together in order to avoid separation. Every effort is now made to place twins together when adoption occurs.

3

Twin Loss Through Death

I T IS SO HARD TO TALK OF DEATH and difficult
to write about, be it about a twin or non-twin. My
research has given me greater understanding of the
pain these twins have known when they have lost, as
many have expressed it, a part of themselves. One twin I
met recently put it this way, "His loss is to me as though
I had lost one of my arms." Here are just a few of the
many comments twins have made to me after I asked
them to respond to the question regarding the possibility
of losing their twin. One said "I don't think it's possible
to prepare yourself and I can't imagine a time when we
will have to deal with it. It's something too hard to think
about." Kathy writes: "I cannot bear the thought of my
twin's death. I am not afraid to die, but don't know how
well I will function if she's not around and I am. I don't
know any way to ease the loss other than deepening my
personal faith and remembering the time spent together.
The memories shared will always be tucked into my
heart." Sharon Johnston wrote: "Develop other

14

relationships, especially a relationship with Jesus Christ. I don't think I could cope with the loss of my twin without comfort from Jesus."

My years of research let me see many changes in my twin participants since they responded to my first questionnaire. I've attempted to locate a twin, only to learn to my dismay from a mother, or other relative, that the twin is now deceased. I have struggled for the right words. Loss of a family member, or friend is always difficult. Death is difficult to accept, whether the death of a twin or non-twin, and only the one experiencing loss can fully know the depth of feeling.

The purpose of this chapter is to help the reader better understand and cope with the loss that twins feel when one of them dies. To read the words of other twins who have suffered loss may give comfort. Many letters I received offered suggestions to twins as to how they can prepare for the inevitable.

It is not for me to say that twins experience more difficulty in accepting the loss of a twin than a singleton in losing a sibling. It might be more traumatic for twins, as they have shared life together before birth and may find separation from their companion devastating.

Twins have not only lost a sibling, they have lost their twin. Many twins, especially identicals, are satisfied to limit much of their time to their twin, often to the exclusion of other siblings and neighborhood children. When death takes one of them, the loss may be even more traumatic because they have failed to create camaraderie and communication with their other siblings and peers-and possibly with their parents.

Of all the human relationships recorded, none are so extraordinary as the ones between identical twins who are parted by death. Several cases have been documented in which a twin, sensing the inevitable death of his stricken twin, has decided to die simultaneously. "Dying to stay together" is rare among the thousands of twins who are separated by death. Far more common are "linked-life" experiences that demonstrate how traumatic and disorienting the loss of a twin can be to the survivor.

In case after case, surviving twins have told of a prescient feeling, a strange uneasiness, a sense of something about to happen, just before their twin was fatally injured or died of an illness. Other twins have expressed a terrible draining away of themselves, a sense of sharp displacement so acute that they became confused as to whether they or their twin had died.

An identical twin, Mona, told of staring at her dead twin lying in her coffin and reaching out to touch her hand. At the moment of contact, Mona said she felt a strange shock go through her and she remembered seeing her own hand become "hazy", as if it were fading away. A few days later in her room looking at herself and her hand in a mirror, Mona started trembling with severe shock. She had the weird feeling that it was she, not her sister, who was dead and the figure in the mirror was not a reflection of herself.

So severe was the feeling of separation from herself that Mona sought psychiatric help at a mental health center. For weeks she received therapeutic counseling, the doctor instructing her to continue to reassure herself. "When you look in the mirror, know that you are looking at yourself and your hand, not your sister and her hand."

Mona required several months of therapy until she adjusted from a double life to a single one. There were many times during the period of her counseling that she was not sure who was dead. Her appearance before a mirror brought on terrible spasms and her body would shake. Eventually, she moved to New York, taking a job as housekeeper at a hospital.

When Mona wrote to me she expressed the hope that the telling of her experience would be helpful to other twins going through the process of adjusting to the death of a twin, the death of part of themselves.

Karrie Bettes knows what it is to receive a premonition about a twin. She and her identical twin sister, Kathy, were having coffee together on Friday, November 11, 1983. They loved to have long talks about old times, friends they shared and their children. Meeting together was a comfortable ritual that both women enjoyed and anticipated. The sisters were particularly close, drawn together to comfort one another after the death of their mother when they were 14.

When Karrie and Kathy finished their coffee and started to leave the restaurant, a strong feeling of dismay came over Karrie. She stared at Kathy, suddenly trying to find a clue to her own apprehension in her sister's face. Something was wrong, but Karrie didn't know what. Reluctantly, she parted with Kathy, pushing aside the uneasiness she felt.

Less than an hour after Karrie had arrived home from the restaurant, she received an urgent call from Kathy's husband.

"Kathy's been in an accident," he said. Karrie rushed to her car and drove madly to the hospital. She learned Kathy had been in a freeway accident and was in critical condition. Her blood pressure was dangerously low, and ten minutes later her heart stopped beating.

After Kathy's death, Karrie tried to avoid going places where her sister had been known. Being mistaken for Kathy hurt Karrie deeply, reminding her of the loss of her twin.

Karrie told me, "A major part of my life and of me was laid to rest when Kathy died. For 23 years one-half of me was her, and I think it always will be. Just as a part of me is gone, a part of Kathy lives on through me." Kathy left a little girl who was two years and ten months old at the time of the accident. Karrie says, "She will have a part of her mommie in me."

Karrie has found comfort in sharing her loss with others who understand. She writes: "If there is any one thing I could say to a twin it would be to take advantage of that bond! Not many people are given another person who fully understands you. You were together the first nine months of life, you're a piece of each other. Don't waste a minute of it. Being a twin is special and you were chosen for that gift.

"It's so sad to think of twins who for some reason or another aren't speaking to their twin. Don't let silly selfish pride keep you from your "gift". Why go through life lonely when a few humble words can bring you the deepest friendship you can ever know.

"Kathy and I had our fights, but the feeling was much like I feel now—a piece missing, lonely, incomplete. Until we resolved our fights I felt incomplete and different. If only a humble word would bring her back, but she's gone from me—forever. Until the Lord decides to take me 'home'. She'll be there. What a reunion!"

The mental rapport between some identical twins is so astonishing that it has been labeled as a form of clairvoyance. If that explanation is unsatisfactory it is because thought transference is unsubstantiated scientifically. Also, nobody really understands how clairvoyance works, much less the sense of "halving," the sudden loss of identity many twins describe when death separates them from their twin. No one knows for certain how thought passes between one person and another. The enigma is fascinating and so are identical twins to ESP researchers because they are the ones who have demonstrated the most extraordinary facility in the exchange of unspoken thoughts.

Parents are perplexed and awed by routine mental exchanges between identical twins who may be separated by thousands of miles.

A mother of identical twin sons reported that Harvey nonchalantly told her one day that his brother Harry, had won a swimming meet at the YMCA. "'How do you know that?' I asked him. Harvey just shrugged. He knew Harry had won before he came home to show off his medal."

Another parent reported her teenage daughter's sudden anxiety one evening. The 14 year-old jumped up from her chair and said positively, "Chandra's been hurt, I think she's broken her wrist."

The identical twin sister was spending the night at a friend's house at a slumber party. A few minutes after Chandra's sister warned that she'd been hurt, the mother of Chandra's friend telephoned to report that Chandra had been taken to the hospital with a broken wrist, suffered when the girls had gotten too rambunctious.

In his book, *Linked Lives*, author Harvey Day reported that twin dancers Jean and Joe Readinger both thought up the identical original dance routine while one was in Chicago and the other was in Pittsburgh. They danced the complicated steps together when they were reunited just as if they had been practicing the routine together for months.

There is very little research on ESP in twins. One of the explanations offered for the paucity of material is that ESP—embracing telepathy, clairvoyance, psychokinesis—does not have enough credibility as a science or discipline of study to attract money to pay for investigators.

This was summarized by Nancy L. Segal, formerly twin research associate in the Department of Psychology at the University of Minnesota, when she wrote "...little progress has been made toward confirming the presence of ESP between twins. Few studies have been attempted and fewer still have found evidence of the phenomenon."

Lack of overwhelming evidence does not change the fact that twin observers who have collected impressive amounts of anecdotal data on psychic transactions between twins are completely convinced of their reliability. They predict that twins who exhibit supersensory communication will open the door to a deeper understanding of thought transference despite the lack of scientific study in the field.

A striking incident demonstrates the strong psychic bond that exists between some twins. In some cases it is so strong that it may precipitate a death signal that both twins may share simultaneously.

Loy Henderson, former United States Ambassador to India, Iran and Iraq, reported a vision in which his brother, Roy, appeared by his bedside while he was lying in a hospital convinced he was near death. Loy and his brother talked of the pain of their parting, then Roy disappeared. Instead of dying, Loy recovered and three days later a cablegram was delivered which announced his brother's death—of an infection following a tooth extraction, at the same instant he had appeared in his brother's farewell vision at the hospital.

If some twins can share ordinary thoughts, duplicate ideas, emulate one another's choices of colors, clothes,

20

cars, choose marriage partners with the same name, even dream alike simultaneously, imagine then the shock to the survivor of the death of a twin. The sense of deprivation may be so fundamental that it may penetrate into the remaining twin's deepest subconscious levels of self awareness. The shock may prove too severe for the survivor to live.

The grief of an identical twin for his absent "other half" goes far beyond the normal sense of loss. It involves the emptiness that results from the destruction of the "couple effect". This phenomenon was identified by Rene Zazzo of the University of Paris, who has been studying twin patterns. Zazzo concluded that traditional methods of studying twins were in error by regarding them as doubles rather than as "couples."

"Only a few of the remarkable peculiarities of twins' development are known for sure," Zazzo observed, "such as delayed intellectual development, language retardation...difficulties related to fragile self-consciousness and sociability."

As a result of Zazzo's concept of two as a couple, other twin researchers began to see that twins had created a priority in their understanding of their own true identities. Ourselves came before myself. Identical twins, especially, think of themselves as one unit, rather than as two persons who look and act alike. This couple definition was buttressed by the science of Chronogenetics which has discovered that some identical twins are fated by their inherited genes to die at the same time of the same disease.

John and Arthur Mowforth, former Royal Air Force pilots who died of heart attacks within the same hour on May 4, 1975, are but one example of dozens of the stunning coincidence of the couple effect in death.

Given the time clock in the genes of many identical twins, and the social, psychological, environmental and psychic dual development of identical twins, it seems apparent that the separation that death brings between the "couple" who are twins is not only shocking to the surviving twin, but actually feels to him as if his body and soul have been severed.

I received a touching letter from Jerry Zimmer in January 1991 which sensitively expressed grief, disorientation, pathos and the physical and psychic yearning through which Jerry passed since his brother Jim died. The letter is printed here with Jerry's permission:

"On December 8, 1985 at 12:39 pm, my twin was killed in a plane crash. At the same time I was ice skating with my two older boys. I discovered later that at the same instant he was killed my body went into a wave of awful shock.

"I instantly ached from head to toe from an awful pain like, maybe, being under a twenty ton pile of rock. I felt like I was being crushed from the outside in. The intensity of this physical discomfort was the same in my eyelids as on my back and toes. It is hard to describe the feeling. Being crushed is as close as I can come to describing it. My voice totally disappeared. I could not talk. I tried, but my vocal cords would not respond to my mental command. This is too hard to explain. It was like being mute. My mouth moved but no sound came out. Days passed before I could talk and many times when I was speaking my voice would suddenly disappear.

"Those pains of grief lasted on and off for over three years. Even today I have them and when I think about Jim my voice goes away. Five years after his death, I have adjusted to the crushing pain and voice loss. When it comes it doesn't last very long and it doesn't happen very often.

"After Jim's death my memory became very good. I could recall our whole life together, every little detail from childhood to being 40 years old. Even today, my memory of Jim and our life together is totally recallable.

"Jim and I were, and still are, best friends. A best friend is a person you can share your most private thoughts with, and he or she can appreciate things spouses can't. They can't share thoughts like identical twins do. Spouses and offspring aren't as good a friend as a twin.

"Never a night or day goes by that I don't think of Jim. I have not had a good night's sleep in five years. He is always at the threshold of my conscious mind. When I meditate and communicate with him, I think I hold both sides of our conversation because I know what he is going to say to me. We never have stopped talking to each other. When Jim and I were alive we worked out all of our problems, big and little together. Now I battle them alone.

"After his death I contemplated suicide thousands of times. I pleaded and prayed to God to take me too. I wanted to be with Jim more than I wanted to live. Those feelings are still with me after five years of his being gone.

"It took four of those five years to come to the reality that Jim was really gone. Thousands of times I would pinch myself or slap myself trying to wake up from the awful dream of his death. I couldn't believe he was really gone.

"I have no close or good friend now, and probably never will. I deeply want my oldest boy to be a little like Jim but he isn't old enough yet to understand my loss.

"The worst thing about Jim being gone is, I have no one to share my thoughts with and my grief. As for how to prepare for a loss like this, I don't know what to do."

Twins seeking consolation and understanding for the long period of grieving and sense of abandonment they feel when they lose a twin have found relief talking with other twins. These veterans of loss realize the death of a twin does not change the relationship for the survivor.

One twin, whom I first met two years ago, was in the depths of depression. She had lost her twin brother at age fifteen. At that time she told me, "I have only a few moments from time to time when I am free from depression, and at the moment, I'm just not all that sure I'm going to make it through."

"More and more I'm having thoughts of suicide," she wrote. This twin is now in her sixties. She said, "Little did I realize just what my life would be like when I lost my twin brother. I feel that my sisters and youngest brother have always been jealous of me because I was a twin." She goes on to say that "No one but another twinless twin ever understands a person who has lost his or her twin and how it has impacted and affected their life. Siblings in a family need to learn to understand the special relationship between twins and not be jealous of their bond."

This woman after seeing a psychiatrist for 25 years has finally realized she needed other ways of handling her problems. She is now taking care of herself through better eating habits and not relying on prescription drugs. She is accomplishing things she never attempted before. She has taken up the cello and has played in her first recital. This twin adds, "I'm making new friends, and taking time to fix up, decorate, and buy new things for my apartment."

She closes her letter by telling me of a statement her twin made that gives her great comfort. She overheard him say to a friend, "She's mine because she's my twin."

4

Twin Loss Through Murder

S INCE SANDRA WAS EDITOR OF THE
Buccaneer, the school newspaper, it was only
natural when the news editor came running up to
her to ask if she wanted him to go to the football field,
which was teeming with people and flashing lights.
Little did she know that her twin had just been murdered
by a stranger on parole.

"My last year of high school was filled with silence.
My friends suddenly vanished. No one talked to me.
They didn't know what to say, not even the teachers. For
me, the second half of my senior year wasn't the carefree
romp ending childhood before striking out as an adult.
Instead it was the beginning of the running."

Says Sandra, "In one long crash course I was forced
to graduate to the world of the monolithic individual, to
the world where "one" means alone. No longer was I one
of the girls. No longer was I even sure that I existed.
After all, Karen no longer did. And without her I was
just a planner without a past."

If my book encourages just one person to learn to respond to someone who has lost a loved one to murder, then all the effort in its writing has not been wasted.

The manner by which someone loses a loved one to death does not diminish the need for comfort, care and listening. Just the presence of loved ones is a statement of care. This is not the only means of expressing care. The look, the gesture, the flowers, the casseroles are all ways we let another person know we care.

I share Sandra's experience of losing a twin to murder because she so openly shares with us her reaction to losing a twin when she was seventeen years old. She tells how she dealt with her loss and how she finally came to accept it and is now getting on with her life. Writes Sandra "I ran from myself and began a long journey of denial rather than face the loss. Instead, I lost my true self. I failed to form my own opinions, decide what I wanted or make close friendships, all to block out the question, 'Who am I now?'"

While Sandra's friends were shopping for prom dresses, Sandra and her mother were shopping for dresses to wear to the grand jury trial. Sandra was shocked when her mother handed her size 16 dresses to try on. "Mother, I'm a size 12. Don't you remember?" It was at that moment that she realized she had gained 25 pounds and gone from size 12 to size 16. Sandra went on to say 'I had run so far away from myself that my own body had become a stranger.'

Sandra goes on to say "I looked forward to going away to college where nobody knew me. In my hometown, my presence reminded people of the murder and that caused them pain. Their faces fell whenever they saw me. I could see the pain in their eyes during our brief conversations. In college I wouldn't shoulder that responsibility. I could be an unknown quantity.

"'Do you have brothers or sisters?' my college roommate asked me as we unpacked and decorated our dorm room. "Brothers."

I plunged into my studies and extracurricular activities and met Mark. We had so much in common. We were studying communications – and each other. I thought I could fill the big hole Karen's death had created in my soul. I came home for Thanksgiving bubbling about Mark.

"Sandy, your clothes are hanging off you!" my mother exclaimed when she saw me arrive at the airport. I hadn't even noticed that I had lost the 25 pounds I had gained earlier that year."

"After graduation we began dating each other and soon started thinking about marriage.

"'Being the wife of a man in radio demands constant moving, every two or three years,' he warned me. 'We'll have to go where the jobs are.'

"'That's OK.' Deep down inside the chance to start new every couple of years excited me. I'd never need to get really close to a community. I'd be so busy learning a new job and meeting new friends that I'd never have to face my thoughts. I could run from this–never have to really think about it.

"Seventeen years have passed. As long without Karen as with her. I now realize that I've been running instead of dealing with the pain of the loss. I stopped denying the loss and I'm able to be aware of my body, opinions and thoughts. I'm now developing a life that includes Karen as a fond memory. I'm not forsaking Karen, instead I'm honoring myself and the life I have to live. "I'm happy," Karen said to me in a dream. "Go on and enjoy yourself."

You may ask why it took Sandra so long to reach the point where she was able to get on with her life. If we were to ask Sandra, she would most likely be hard pressed to answer the question. Grieving is a very personal process and is handled differently by each person. So many circumstances and events can advance or inhibit the healing process. The right words from the right person at the right time can make a big difference. I'm happy to report that in the last few years great advances have been made in behalf of those who are grieving. Many resources available to twins are listed in the back of the book.

"You must attend the National POMC conference if at all possible," Martha Johnson said to me. I didn't know what she was talking about. I was soon to learn that POMC is the acronym for Parents of Murdered Children. And I was to learn that Martha Johnson, the mother of three sets of twins, had lost one of her twin daughters to murder. At her insistence I decided to attend the next conference which was held in Concord, California in August, 1993.

There I met with over 200 parents who had lost their children to murder. Several of the children were twins.

POMC was founded by Charlotte and Bob Hullinger, whose daughter was murdered in 1978. Charlotte said, "It began out of our personal need, not out of any altruistic motives." I am delighted to report that POMC has been able to give support to over 38,000 survivors throughout the United States and abroad.

At this conference I found loving and compassionate people from all walks of life who were there to let others know that they understood the pain they were experiencing. They were there to give strength to others.

With permission from the National Organization of

Parents of Murdered Children, Inc. I am able to share with you some of their thoughts on coping:

First, don't be surprised at the strong emotions that come: shock, disbelief, anger toward the murderer, frustration with justice delayed or denied, seeming loss of faith in God and people.

Second, expect to be numb, confused, depressed or unable to stop crying. Sometimes survivors have difficulty releasing their emotions. You may feel as if you are losing your sanity, but you're probably not. These are normal reactions.

Third, it is natural to experience a primal kind of fear. Childhood fears of the "bogeyman" coming in the middle of the night and murdering you become real.

Fourth, be gentle with yourself. Grief takes much longer to resolve than most people realize. It affects the body as well as the emotions.

Fifth, as much as you may want to do it, don't build a wall around yourself. You are not alone and being involved with others will help your recovery, especially if you can channel your strong emotions into constructive action.

Under the resources listed in the back of the book you will find POMC listed with their telephone number. They are there to help you.

Darcie D. Sims, a psychotherapist and grief management specialist, who lives in Albuquerque, New Mexico, was a workshop speaker at the POMC conference in Concord, California. Her workshop was titled *Humor in the Grieving Process*. With great compassion and understanding she addressed parents who had lost their children to murder. Her words brought both tears and laughter as she walked them through various stages in the grieving process. She continued to stress that grief is the price we pay for love. She said "In the midst of your darkest moment, in any moment of whatever you're doing that brings the greatest moment of pain, I want you to stop and put in your mind the smile that makes it hurt so bad. Humor is the greatest source of tears because it says "Somebody loved me.' Let me say again, grief is the price we paid for love. You paid that price." She also went on to say, "Pain and hurt expand the spirit. The broken places don't get healed by filling them up, but by understanding that it expands the spirit. You can begin to love and love again."

Dr. Sims' books on grief management are listed in the resources in the back of this book.

Martha Johnson tells her story in hopes that by her telling, it will help others who may experience such a loss.

Martha writes: "My world fell apart on Feb 28, 1983. Oh how I hate the month of February. I never got to say good-bye and I love you. The day of the twenty eighth started out the same as always: up at five, I got ready for work and then got my youngest son Bobby ready for school.

"I went out to get the newspaper and turned to the local section. The article on February 28, 1983 read "Body Found In Woods." I had a very bad feeling when I read it. My daughter Ada had been missing since the 9th of February, and from the description of the person I had a very bad feeling. I called our local Sheriff's department and they said they would call back. "I don't really remember what they said, but I think it was "Yes, Mrs. Johnson, it's your daughter. I remember people coming and going. It was a living hell on earth. All the questions. We were all suspects. They asked me if I was sure she was home the night of the eighth and then, "How do you know?" I lost my child, why couldn't they just leave me and my family alone. It took over a year to find her murderer. Not knowing made it hard on all of us. I didn't trust anyone and I was scared for my other children. What hurts so much is that she died alone, left in the woods. I never got to say good-bye.

"The helplessness that I felt for her surviving twin Susie is something that really bothered me. My heart broke for her. Susie didn't and still doesn't want to talk about it. She says that nobody understands. Part of her is missing. I know she hurts because part of me is part of them. Ada and Susie are fraternal twins but they had a closeness that only twins can share: nine months of togetherness that they have alone. Susie is lost. And I hurt when I see her hurt.

"Holidays are bad. We celebrate but it's so hard. Susie feels left out because Cheryl and Tina, also twins, have each other and are together. We have a link missing from our family chain and that chain was broken by my Ada's murder."

Martha goes on to say, "Mom's and Dad's hurt twice. Once for their loss and again for the living twin whose world has been destroyed. I spoke at a Compassionate Friends meeting one night. A few student nurses were in the group. I had one young girl come up to me after, with tears in her eyes and she told me, 'Thank you. I'm a twin and I loved my sister but I didn't know how much until I heard you talk about your daughter. I even thought of killing myself at one time. It's hard to talk about. I hated myself and I blamed myself because I was not there to protect her and love her when she died."

I asked Martha what she does that helps her deal

with her loss. She shared this:

"I keep a journal of how I feel and have since 1983. I also write Ada (the daughter who was murdered) and let her know how much we love her and how much we miss her. I love my children so much and all of it goes in my journal. I have had people say I know you don't want to talk about it, but we do want to talk about our loved ones. We want their memories kept alive because we still love our children. Another thing I do is the lighting of four candles on all holidays, birthdays and date of death. The lighting of the candles was sent out to all POMC members from the National Parents of Murdered Children a few years ago and every Christmas when I send out my cards I put a copy in the card. Our organization is a self-help support group. POMC is an organization you would like not to have but thank God we have it and the sad part is we grow everyday. With time you heal but the hurt never goes away."

Following is the candlelight memorial which she sent:

"The first candle represents our grief. The pain of losing them is intense. It reminds us of the depth of our love.

"The second candle represents our courage–to confront our sorrow–to comfort each other–to change our lives.

"The third candle is in their memory–the times we laughed, the times we cried, the times we were angry with each other–the caring and joy you gave us.

"The fourth candle denotes love. As we enter this season, day by day, we cherish the special place in our hearts that will always be reserved for them. We thank them for the gift their lives brought to each of us."

"I have a great fear that my surviving twin daughter

33

will not make it," one mother told me. This mother lost her other twin daughter to murder, and the remaining twin daughter has not been able to overcome the devastating loss of losing her twin sister. The story is not yet finished for at this time we are in the process of pulling together resources which hopefully will give the needed support to this grieving twin. This mother is doing all she can to find support for herself during this time of loss and is an active participant in POMC. She is doing all she can to give the support which will help her remaining twin daughter survive the loss of her twin sister.

5

Twin Loss Through Suicide

OFTEN IT IS THE SURVIVING TWIN who is able to make the most accurate assessment of why a twin resorted to suicide, since the communication between them is often so total in sharing, and their childhood experiences so alike.

Carolyn Angle, an identical twin, has shared with us about the loss of her twin to suicide, in the hopes that the coping methods that she chose will help other twins in their time of grief.

"You asked what caused Marilyn to kill herself. Looking back with the insight I have gained the last three years, I believe it was the severe abuse, incest, and sexual molestations we endured. I developed multiple personality disorder as a means of survival and I believe Marilyn did too. Unfortunately her psychiatrists did not pick up on this and one of the more depressed personalities was persistent enough to be successful.

"Coping has been very difficult. I carried a few grains of her ashes with me for many years. There were

35

a few granules of ashes in the wrapping paper when I unwrapped the urn so I put them in a pink envelope and carried it with me for many years. I still have the envelope.

"Someone told me lighting a candle can be very helpful. I made a special shopping trip to pick out just the right candle. Marilyn loved lace, crystal and pink, so I bought a beautiful lace doily, a crystal candle holder and the largest (so it would last a long time) pink candle I could find. The soft flickering light was comforting. I drew pictures of the feelings I could not express in words. When I first got into effective therapy I wrote a letter to Marilyn which reads in part:

"Dear Marilyn,

It's been eleven years since you took your own life and I still feel the pain as if it were yesterday. Hardly a day goes by that I don't wish you were here. There are so many things I want to tell you. So many things I want to share with you.

"I'm so sad that you felt killing yourself was the only way out. If you could have hung on a little longer. I know so much more about why we had so much pain, anger, and depression in our lives. I feel angry and cheated that your doctors didn't know what was wrong and didn't care enough to find out instead of just drugging you and providing the tool for the hopelessly desperate part of you to use to stop the pain within.

"How I wish I could have been there for you. I was so enmeshed in my own pain that I could not see how desperate you were. I love you Marilyn. It's a lonely life without you. We had so little time to know one another, we were so filled with pain and anger.

"I truly hope your pain and anger are gone now and you are happy and at peace with yourself.

"Much love, Carolyn.

"P.S. Give Momma a hug and kiss for me."

"As our fiftieth birthday approached I was really struggling to cope. I wanted something very special to commemorate this milestone. Ed Nelson, a very dear man who happens to be a therapist and in particular specializes in bereavement, offered to help me find a way to cope.

"I wanted something very special to commemorate this milestone. Many times through the years Mama, Marilyn and I had discussions about death and dying. Mama believed money and flowers were for the living. She wanted to be cremated and her ashes scattered on the ocean. Marilyn and I wanted to be the same as Mama. We promised ourselves and each other that when the time came we would do this for each other. No power on earth or in heaven could have stopped me from making sure this happened for my twin."

"My Marilyn loved jewelry and diamonds in particular. While my husband and I were overseas we had purchased several nice pieces of jewelry at considerable discount. I took the pieces to a jeweler and traded them for a gold bangle bracelet with channel set diamonds. On the inside I had engraved 'For Carolyn's fiftieth birthday in memory of Marilyn, 6-11-40 to 1-25-79.'

"In addition, Ed helped me plan and took his personal time for a memorial service. I bought some pink lacy carnations, baby's breath, paper and ribbons and made a small bouquet for each of Marilyn's three sons and my two sons and one for myself. I wrote cards for each of the boys with what I thought they might want to say to their mother or aunt. I also wrote a letter to Marilyn from me.

"My husband B.J., Kimberley Deaton, a special girlfriend of mine, Ed Nelson and I drove almost three hours to where I rented a boat. We took the flowers out into the ocean and had a memorial service. It was a perfect day! A gray, overcast sky was drizzling soft rain, and the wind was kicking up whitecaps and rolling swells. It was a great ride out. I know Ed and B.J. were freezing and wet but they did not complain. They just stood beside me in the bow and we dipped and bounced in and out of the waves. Marilyn would have loved it. I loved it too. I felt her presence!

"The pilot stopped the boat and I read each card before laying the flowers on the water. After I had read my letter and laid my flowers on the water, Ed added a single red rose he had brought with him. I was so touched that he would take his whole Sunday to be with me and bring a single red rose for a lady he never knew! Wow! That was quite a gift–Thank you, Ed. You will always have a special place in my heart!

"The ride back to shore was as bouncy and wet as it was going out. It was a wonderful day filled with lots of healing.The experience helped immensely to ease my pain and sorrow. I still miss her very much but it is not so painful.

"Last year I made arrangements with the nearby children's park to place a bench in memory of Marilyn. The plaque reads, 'In loving memory of my identical twin sister, Marilyn Ray Culbertson Sanders. Toxic shame took your life and robbed us of your time. 6-11-40 to 1-25-79'."

This is the letter Carolyn wrote to Marilyn for the memorial service.

"Dear Marilyn,

"Tomorrow we turn fifty and you ought to be here to

celebrate with me. I feel so cheated! These could have been some of our best years. We could have been terrorizing the mall, haunting every jewelry store within a hundred miles and giggling like idiots over mounds of ice cream piled high with whipped cream and cherries.

"I miss you so much. I catch my reflection in a shop window and know something is missing...where's the second reflection–so like the first?

"You were a terrific teacher. I still shave my legs, fuss with my hair and feel uncomfortable without makeup. You were more like a big sister teaching me the ways of a young lady. You were always the leader, pushing me into adventures I would never have dared on my own.

"Who's going to teach me to be a classy old lady?

"Much love, Carolyn"

Each time I have contact with these wonderful twins who have lost their twin, I am once again refreshed by the strength they exhibit. I find joy in seeing their determination to turn sorrow into rejoicing and continuing to remember the precious times they shared in their togetherness.

Deborah, an identical twin, spent years trying to support and at the same time help her twin become independent. Deborah is trying to come to terms with the death of her sister. She writes: "When I visit her, I visit her near the seashore at a cemetery located on the north side of town. The memories of our life together begin to unfold in my mind. I think about our childhood, our teenage years and our struggle with adulthood. Suddenly, I realize I must carry on our childhood dreams and wishes without her. As I turn to leave it's hard to believe that she's gone, and not at my kitchen table drinking coffee with me and talking about our future.

"Growing up as a twin was like looking into a looking glass, for my twin sister and I looked a great deal alike. When Dana and I reached the age of seventeen the looking glass began to shatter into tiny pieces that increased over the years, until one day when it finally shattered and fell tumbling to the ground. We were no longer one and our childhood dreams and wishes were hidden and forgotten in the back of our minds. We were faced with an identity crisis that we both continued to struggle with for the next fifteen years. She lived her separate life drowning her soul in alcohol and drugs, while I chose to move away and start my life anew. With a new life and a separate identity, I fought the withdrawals of alcohol and drugs and it changed my life forever. I wanted more out of my life than being Dana's twin and doing the wrong things in life."

It is uncertain whether the overdose was accidental or intentional. Dana's family is still struggling with the questions that inevitably accompany such a troubled life and tragic ending.

If you find that you are feeling suicidal, realize that it is only a reaction to the pain of loss, and it will pass. If you have any serious thoughts of acting on these feelings, seek professional help at once. Call an operator and ask for the suicide prevention agency. Tell him it is an emergency.

6

Separation & Reuniting

S OME MOVING TESTIMONY has been recorded by surviving twins who insist they will not allow death to force them to relinquish the distinction of being a twin. They consider themselves to be "separated" twins who will be reunited with their missing twin at some point in the future after their own death.

Paula Jean (Bingham) Crosse understands what it is to face the loss of a twin. "When did the 'turning point' come? I'm not sure," writes Paula. "Was it when the realization of her singular pain came into my consciousness? Or when that compulsion to 'go it alone' entered the forefront of my mind? It created a moment of crisis when it dawned on me that her demise was sure to come.

"Being born twins is a unique experience. Looking alike, dressing alike, being mistaken for one another right up through our 10th birthdays created an existence unlike most others. It got to the point that a dress purchased, a person visited, a decision made–could not be completed without one another's consultation."

Paula recognized that she had not pulled on strengths that were hers before her twin died. It is sad that it often takes a loss or estrangement for a twin to feel liberated and strong.

After losing her twin sister, Paula faced her future. "And now? Finding oneself. Knowing one's capabilities. Finding sudden joy in knowing that I could attempt something: an assignment at work, writing poems, accomplishing a new weight-loss program, all without the twin-oriented dependence. Laughter coming easily (it never did before). A new person discovering capabilities and potential never known before.

Paula continues, "My son, family and I are still coming to terms with living without Donna. Her personality, her zest for living, her example of living with a handicap (as opposed to living a handicapped life), her inspiration, the total all-encompassing medical burdens that Momma and the family tried to cope with. All that is gone now. And it would seem that we all became a little giddy with the sudden freedom from those burdens. But it was not really that way. It was, instead, nerves that had been strung out too long, almost snapping from the tension, that were being played out in almost frenetic activity. But we have all settled down, come down to earth. Now fond memories enter the picture: a remembrance of Donna smiling at something, laughing at one of our jokes, combing Danny's hair, giving Paula sisterly/motherly advice. Or looking through a box in the storage room and finding a photograph of Donna–fond memories of a sweet, gentle-nurtured, hurting young girl/woman. Donna and Paula: once twins, now separated. And one day, we will be joined together again."

Raymond W. Brandt, Ph.D., EDD, of Fort Wayne,

Indiana, founder of the Twinless Twins Support Group International, beautifully expressed the confidence of the surviving twin in the ultimate reunion when he wrote:

"I remember distinctly how I knew the exact moment when my twin was accidentally electrocuted on an electric transmission line pole. A strange, indescribable feeling overwhelmed me. I knew my twin's soul had left his physical body and my soul felt like joining his. I yearned to be with him where he had gone, but my life on earth continued on. When my death does come, I know I will not be disappointed. I will be on my merry way to join my identical twin—join myself as it were, and become a wholeness once again."

The loss of a twin also affects other members of the family in a different way than the death of a child who is a singleton. Much of the adjustment to the loss will depend on how the twins related to one another and to other members of the family. Age of the twin at death is also a major factor.

Because of the burden of grief and the decisions that have to be made at the time of death, parents often fail to assist the surviving twin with his emotions. Involved in their own hurt, they forget the remaining twin's deeper anguish. He can suffer two losses as the result of his twin's demise—the loss of his twin and the temporary loss of support of his parents.

Dr. Brandt wrote, "My family seemed to go through usual phases of mourning with no particular support to me as a twin. My twinship was buried with my identical twin and it was not until 1985 that I rediscovered my twinship. As an infantry combat soldier in Korea in 1951, twice seriously wounded, I must never have mentioned to buddies that I was a twin for when I visited one of them in 1986 and mentioned my twin, he was surprised, saying, 'All the time we were together in combat you never mentioned your twin.' The thousands of times, in privacy, I have screamed with the pain of the physical absence of my twin. A twinless twin does not expect a non-twin to understand the pain of being one-half alive and one-half dead.

"As each twinless twin discovers his or her own means of bereavement management there is one thing they must keep before them. They are still a twin! Born a twin, always a twin. Your twin's death did not end your twin status. To end being a twin is a death itself-believe one who suffered it for 36 years."

7

Bonding Through Suffering

P arents of twins need to support the surviving twin emotionally. Each parent develops an individual relationship with a child, and each parent will react to the loss in a different way. This may lead to marital strain if the mother and the father fail to meet the other's expectation for grief or support. This family strain will certainly affect the surviving twin.

If parents have made "twin parenthood" an essential part of their own self image and have difficulty adjusting to the idea of one instead of two, the surviving twin may see himself as having little worth as a single child. This can be a difficult time for him. He may feel excluded from his parent's grief, particularly if they act as if grieving is a silent, personal affair and never talk about the lost twin, or remove all evidence of his existence, creating a ghost.

In this case, the surviving twin cannot express his own grief, guilt or anger. He may even interpret his parents' actions as a silent accusation of blame for his twin's death. Unless he can get help to resolve his feelings, he may carry his twin's ghost well into adulthood.

Parents often fear that they also will lose their surviving child. This is particularly acute if the twins were young, or if the ailment was one that had a genetic base. Parents may become overprotective and give the surviving twin the message that life is full of danger. The twin may become timid and afraid of any physical or emotional separation from his mother and father. Interdependence may interfere with the formation of other relationships, especially with the opposite sex. Some children may react to this unhealthy parental smothering by openly defying danger and inviting parental punishment.

Seeking to replace the lost twin by transferring all of their expectations for the lost child onto his surviving twin can also be devastating for that remaining twin. Encouraged to live for two, the survivor may take on some personality traits of his lost twin. He may also try to fill the empty place by engaging in activities in which his twin excelled.

The other factor that would affect the parents' grief and the actions of the surviving twin are the circumstances of the death. If the death was sudden, the surviving twin may identify with the pain and try to relive the event in his nightmares. Possibly, he may feel guilty that he survived or that he was not able to prevent the death. The way in which the surviving twin reacts to the death of his twin will depend on how close the two were.

Caroline Tancredy, an identical who lost her twin to a sudden illness, had discussed death with her twin. She wrote: "My sister Mary and I did almost everything together. Of course there were times when we were not side by side, but we were always aware of what the other one was doing, and we knew we had each others' unconditional support. As twins, we had a deep personal understanding of one another's thoughts and feelings. I have never been able to accurately describe this understanding to a non-twin, but I feel that it is some sort of sixth sense. In a way I feel as if I know Mary better than I know myself.

"As a twin I have been given a very unique and special gift: I was born into life with a partner. This partner would learn with me, grow with me, discover life's joys with me, and hold my hand through life's disappointments.

"Above all, I had the security of knowing that I would never be alone, and that my partner would always love me. Of course Mary and I realized that although we were born together, we would probably not die together. Thought of such a severe separation scared us, and we decided to conquer it.

"As Catholics we believed in a place called heaven, but we weren't sure of its rules. We often talked about the mysteries of death and we made a pact to cover our bases. Our promise stated: I will never leave you, even if I die. If it is possible to visit you after I have died (through dreams or in spirit) I will. I will watch you, protect you, and guide you because I love you.

"If this promise sounds childlike, it is because we were children when we made it. At age seven Mary and I learned about death. Growing up we spent almost every weekend at my grandma's house. Her house was a palace to us. She had a big backyard with every kind of fruit tree, a flower garden, a vegetable garden, a vast grassy lawn, a little path surrounding it, just big enough for the two of us and our red Radio Flyer wagon to travel on."

One day Caroline and Mary found an injured bird, and took it to their grandmother. She told them it had died and they decided to bury it. They put the little bird in a box. "Mary held the two pieces of wood, and I hammered them together with the nail to make a cross. We stood under the apple tree, held hands, and said a prayer, "Dear God, please let this birdie fly with you in the sky. Please watch this place, and bless this cross."

"My twin sister Mary died last March, after she became suddenly ill at school. I was fortunate enough to be at her bedside when she passed away. Although she was unconscious at the time, I believe that she could hear me say, "Don't forget our promise, Mary. I love you."

"I also believe that she has kept our promise. Shortly after she died, I was taking a walk around my grandma's backyard and I paused at the apple tree. There, beneath the branches, stood a crooked, weathered cross. I prayed, 'Dear God, please let my sister Mary rest with you in Heaven. Please watch over this place, and bless this cross...and thank you for the gift of memories.'"

Caroline wrote a beautiful and touching account of a dream about her twin. "I am outside of my body, watching the river. Something seems strange and I notice that there are no sounds. I see the water descending the calm, swift slope but I can't hear it. There is Mary coming over the highest point of the river, which is like a gentle waterfall, with sudden, safe drops. I follow shortly after her and notice that we only seem to be nine years old; young faces, small bodies. Then other children come behind us. All of a sudden I am inside my body. The river carries me gently. It is so beautiful and clear that I can see the bottom. I feel at ease in its simplicity and basicness. The river carries my Mary to the next level and, as I come down the slope to join her, I notice that she is splashing in the water and swimming to go further. She never looks back. I think, "What is your rush Mary? The river will carry you and you will get to the bottom eventually." I let the river carry me as Mary goes ahead. She goes over the next level and I can't see her anymore because the drop is steeper. I feel a little panicked as I drop to the next level after her. This time the water is deeper and I sink under and then come up. All of a sudden I feel my age of twenty. The water is no longer shallow and I am scared. Where is Mary? I can't find her. The river does not carry me anymore. I am actually in some sort of cloudy pond. I look beyond the pond and I see a vast, mighty ocean. The waves beat against the pond as if it is the shore. Is Mary out there? I am afraid to go forward, and I am afraid to fall behind. I am afraid to stay where I am. I feel all alone. Abandoned. Did Mary go into that unknown, or is she here somewhere? Am I supposed to follow her? Does she need me to be where she is, or to stay where I am? I don't know where to go and suddenly the water that once embraced me terrifies me.

"When I first woke from this dream I didn't think much about it. But unlike most dreams, which are easily forgotten at the sound of an alarm clock, it lingered in my mind all day. I began to feel that this dream came from the center of my being. Over and over again, I replayed the images: flowing with the river, watching Mary swim ahead of me, falling into the cloudy pond, looking for Mary frantically, and wondering where to go.

"My whole life I have been content to go where life takes me. Even as a child I was aware that life may take

49

me to places I would not choose to go; places I would be afraid of. Yet I was confident that I would survive these tribulations based on one fact: my twin sister Mary would guide me, support me, or protect me. I felt that I was born into life with the tools to conquer its challenges. Mary had the same confidence with a twist. She was not content to 'go with the flow.' She wanted to create her own flow. She took risks, knowing that I was just a short distance behind her to help if she got caught in the current. I followed her in my own style, knowing it was safe to go where Mary went.

"Since Mary's death my whole world has become clouded. I have become overwhelmed with fears of isolation and abandonment. In a sense, I search for her. I surround myself with pictures, talk about her constantly, relive memories, and share every thought and prayer with her. Despite my efforts to survive, I feel that it is not natural to be physically separated from her. In fact, it seems terribly wrong. I keep thinking, "I am going to die because Mary and I must always be together." On the one hand, I feel a separation from Mary that causes physical pains in my chest. On the other hand, I have never felt closer to her, as we are now joined by a spiritual bond which is unique to us.

"Perhaps my dream, which seems full of questions, is actually ripe with answers. I am not at a point in life where the river will carry me. I cannot physically follow my sister into safe waters. My decisions are not clear, and my being is not basic. Perhaps by knowing what is no longer true, I can define the elements of my life which will always remain constant. I cannot see Mary, but she remains with me. We are still a part of the same body of water. And although I cannot swim in her ocean, I have nineteen years of her example to follow to know

the best way to swim: to splash, and go forward with a
love for life, making my own currents, and taking my
own risks. This task is a scary one. Sometimes it is
lonely.

   "As twinless twins, we have not lost our tool. When
the tide crashes against the shore of our being, and the
waters threaten to drown our spirits, we must simply
block out the sound and remember the one basic element
that matters: we share our soul and our ultimate love
with our twins, and our union with them will give us the
strength to endure and, above all, to love life until we are
called into the great, vast ocean."

   Caroline wrote this poem in memory of Mary.

   Dear Mary,

   I was so scared to lose you,
       I prayed you'd make it through
   And at the time God took you,
       I prayed He'd take me too.

   You were all my heart could ask for -
       a sister and a friend
   -always there to guide me
       and a fighter til the end.

   When days are hard and nights are long and
       I'm too weak to cry
   come to me in dreams and
       we'll pretend you didn't die.

We'll take wagon rides in Grandma's yard.
We'll laugh, then laugh some more
And when morning comes we'll say good-bye
and part at heaven's door.

And through the day when I am lost
and I don't know what to do
I'll close my eyes and say a prayer
and trust you'll guide me through.

Love, Caroline

Caroline's mother Paula Tancredy had to come to terms with losing her daughter Mary and then with learning that her daughter Caroline has the same illness and will need treatment for the disease indefinitely.

Paula's twin daughters always had a close relationship. After the death of her daughter Mary, Paula had to learn to establish communication with her daughter Caroline.

Paula writes, "Her sudden loss has had, and continues to have, a profound effect on me and on my family. It has been a year since her death, and the stone cast upon the water continues to ripple through myself and my family.

"After my daughter died I drove into grief-land full throttle. I was disoriented, numb, frantic, disorganized, hurt, lonely, desperate, despairing, alienated. My trust in many things, including myself, disintegrated. I couldn't face my family's grief. I couldn't console them or offer them any words of wisdom to help them with their grief. I have never felt so hopelessly helpless in my life. The pain was constant and disabling.

"In the waiting room of the intensive care unit, as we waited and prayed and wept, I would look at my daughter Caroline, and in my mind reeled with positive certainty that whatever was wrong with my daughter Mary, Caroline would have it too.

"Nineteen years ago I gave birth to identical twin girls. One egg had split by some miracle to separate into two unique individuals that would bond. I had no way of knowing how deeply they would affect each other, blending their personalities, becoming the steel support of each other's being.

"Mary and Caroline would shake their cribs until they were in close enough proximity to one another to climb over the rail and snuggle up with one another. They were joyous with each other's company.

"I would search the library shelves for anything pertaining to raising twins. The tomes dealing with twins were mostly statistical data compiled by singletons who hadn't had a clue as to what were the problems and trials faced on an everyday basis by parents who don't realize what they are dealing with in the first place.

"I watched like a spectator as their individual personalities began to be more pronounced. I was amazed that two people who looked so much alike, raised in the same household and offered the same opportunities, could be so different.

"I think I began to understand a little of how incredibly strong their bond to each other was the first day of school. What I had expected was tears and protests to take them home. What I received was the view of two small forms' backsides, hand-in-hand, that didn't even turn to wave good-bye. I was crushed. It gave me an insight into where I fit into the general parenting picture.

"Mary and Caroline were accepted at different colleges, Mary at Chico State and Caroline at U.C. Davis. Part of the application process included writing an essay on any subject. It shouldn't have surprised me but that they both wrote on the subject of the difficulty of establishing an identity when one is an identical twin."

Mary suddenly became ill and was taken home. Tests at a hospital determined that she needed a liver transplant. Soon she had slipped into a coma and never regained consciousness. Her mother wrote "When at last all hope was extinguished, my husband, Caroline and Elaina, my youngest daughter, all said their good-byes. I stayed with my baby. I felt that I was there when I brought her into this world, I couldn't leave her when she left it. I feel she went from my embrace to God's. I have to believe this or I'd go insane. Totally and utterly insane.

"After we buried Mary, we received a call from the physician who cared for Mary stating it was urgent he talk with us about the autopsy findings. They had discovered that Mary had succumbed to Wilson's Disease, a rare genetic disorder. Her doctor had no doubt that Caroline definitely, and Elaina possibly, had the same disorder." Tests confirmed that Caroline has Wilson's Disease, and she started a course of lifelong medication to control it.

Caroline's mother felt that Caroline was pulling away from her. "Caroline resisted therapy. She withdrew into herself and her memories. The more I reached out to pull her close, the more she retreated, or so it seemed to me."

"She decided to go back to school. I couldn't believe it! My heart broke. I couldn't bear to have her away from me. I needed to look at her, touch her, protect her.

Caroline must have felt smothered at home. She has told me that she went back to school to grieve by herself. I couldn't help but wonder as I watched her drive away if I would ever see her again. It happened once, it could happen again. I pestered her with phone calls. I needed to hear her voice, to know that she was taking her medication. I encouraged her to seek a therapist in proximity of her school.

"It is difficult in the best of times for me not to step in and fix things. As a medical professional, part of my job is assessment and problem solving. It is difficult for me to not carry over this role in dealing with my family. I realize this child of mine is striving to be a woman. She is capable of assessing her own needs. She is struggling with her independence from parental intervention. Now at nineteen she had the awesome burden of separation from the one person she trusted implicitly, loved unreservedly and supported unconditionally.

"My little girl needed help, but who? Who would offer help that could be effective? She finally agreed to a professional therapist. I obtained one for her immediately. But who could she turn to that would most likely understand her twin loss? Another twin is the most logical answer. But where to find such a resource? I contacted theNational Organization of Mothers of Twins Clubs Inc. and within 15 minutes they gave me the name of Dr. Raymond W. Brandt.

"Years ago he had formed a club for 'Twinless Twins.' I contacted them and they put Caroline on their mailing list. Dr. Brandt called Caroline directly and encouraged her to join. I was greatly relieved when Caroline enthusiastically joined this group. Finally there were others who could truly empathize with Caroline's plight.

"I can say with honesty that my greatest source of comfort has come from individuals who have suffered a similar loss. Others who have not lost their child can feel sorrow at your misfortune, know you are in pain, are thankful and praise God that they are not in your position, but no one can realize or share your unendurable agony more than someone who has experienced this loss themselves. I have become very sensitive to the well of human misery that surrounds us and am awed by the resilience of the human spirit.

"Caroline has also received tremendous support from her roommates at school. Each of these young women who live in a small apartment off campus has suffered the loss of a loved one very recently, all of them 'sudden.' Why these young women cast their lot with each other before these events took place must be divine intervention. They allow each other the opportunity to grieve openly or privately. They have given permission to each other to choose the path of their own grief journey. They don't change the subject or try to cheer each other or occupy every moment with tasks or entertainment. They allow each other to validate their pain and sorrow. These are all ways to avoid the pain of grief.

"Shortly after Mary's death I worked myself into a frenzy of activity. I didn't run away, only to my backyard. My daughter Caroline ran to school, my husband back to work. I would have sold my soul to rid myself of the pain of grief and guilt.

"As time passed, I kept a journal. I wanted to remember every little detail. My mind couldn't concentrate long enough to read, but I could write down my thoughts. I'm still keeping a written diary. My memory fails me but my journal is there, concrete and safe for me to express my fears, doubts, prayers and mourning.

"Caroline's comments to me gave me great concern. I worried over the state of her mental health. I have come to realize that all the worry in the world cannot take her away from the grief work we must all perform for ourselves. It is indeed a lonesome valley. I believe we sink into our own private hell and hopefully emerge a better person.

"I have been in discussion with Caroline's therapist and accept that she is qualified to assess Caroline carefully. I've been in touch with her medical doctor and he gives me reassurance that Caroline is strong enough mentally and physically to withstand this emotional and physical upheaval in her life. I need their reassurance. It is my lifebuoy. It seems to me that Caroline will survive this trauma only if she concludes that she has value. That her 'work' here on earth is not complete.

"The greatest fear that Mary and Caroline shared while together, they would fantasize, would be separation by death. She discussed this in an article she wrote for the *Twinless Twins Newsletter*.

"Her future has been altered, and the dreams she shared with her sister shattered. I recently heard a poem which compared the soul to a pane of glass. When we suffer a severe loss, the glass is shattered. The pieces that form the structure of our personality refuse to be pieced together in the same pattern because the person who is 'lost' to us is in each piece. It is the grief work of the individual to piece together a glass that is supported with the framework of faith, family, friends, and time and trust.

"Caroline has stated to me how she not only has to deal with resolving her relationship with Mary past, present and future, but has to create new personality traits within herself to deal with aspects that Mary once provided for her in order to be a whole person again.

"The trip through grief-land is a very difficult, winding, treacherous road. The relationship you share with the loved one is unique, therefore the grieving process for each of us is unique. I have concluded that it is a place where one dwells until their dying day. That the resolved relationship, as many grief authors term it in the many books I have read on the subject, is when you take your last breath.

"There is an upside to grieving. With the incapacity, the time is made available to become introspective, to evaluate, to make decisions about our relationships and our lives and its course in general.

"'What are my goals? Where am I going? Where have I been? What have I learned? What gives my life meaning? Who and what is important to me? Where can I make a difference?' These are questions my daughter Mary left me to ponder as her final gift. I treasure her memory. In her short life she taught me more about living than any book. She wanted to be a teacher. She reached that goal with more impact than those in the profession rarely realize.

"I have adopted the expression my daughters used frequently, 'I can make a difference.' If Mary can no longer be here to make the difference I know she was capable of making, then I will do it for her.

"Caroline's Wilson's Disease is controlled with medication she must take daily for the rest of her life. Her auto immune system is depressed by the mechanism of action of this drug, so her health must be closely monitored by a skilled health care professional. She must learn to be her own advocate as so few have knowledge of her disease. She is learning the art of consumerism in the medical field.

"She is being guided by a therapist skilled in grief therapy to guide her through the labyrinth of feelings. Caroline has given her therapist and me the opportunity to talk about her progress to fine tune her therapy to the best advantage.

"I have come to believe that nothing in this life is accidental. Too many opportunities have come my way at just the right time to be considered fate or accidental. I point to an occurrence that has happened recently. I was home ill and received a call from Mrs. Betty Jean Case inquiring if Caroline might give her permission to print the poem Caroline wrote for Mary. Mrs. Case asked me to write of my experiences and I began work on this paper. I had a divine inspiration to send the rough draft to Caroline for her perusal prior to sending it on to Mrs. Case.

"The flurry of activity that followed caught me by surprise. Caroline, whose avenues of communication varied from non-existent to noncommittal-literally shut down for repair-soon opened wide and a flood of words came from her. We've written to each other explaining actions and words too painful to reveal face-to-face. We've talked for hours exploring each other's feelings in a field grown fallow by lack of communication. In time this field will be carefully cultivated to grow flowers again.

"We are in the process of building a new relationship. Even though we have a lifetime of mutual experiences, we perceived them differently. For the first time I am really beginning to know her.

"I learned that I can't fix everything. I can't assure my daughter Caroline of every happiness. I can only support, love and listen to her. I have learned a very hard lesson in humility. I have acknowledged how vulnerable and fragile we all are in our human condition, and how little control we have over events. I have been taught by my children how precious and valuable each person who touches our lives is. I have tried to embrace my faith and take the sustenance it offers.

"A friend offered these words of comfort the day I buried my daughter: 'God cried the day your daughter died.' It brought home the fact that I was not alone in my grief and sorrow. In the compassion of Christ I have found strength to endure."

Parental support is essential with very young children. Children under five usually have very little understanding of death and what it means. The surviving twin may insist on taking his brother's place. He may sit at the table where his brother sat or take over his teddy bear or other toys. He may carry on conversations with his dead twin and include him with his drawings of the family. Often the surviving twin even fantasizes about his own death as a way of finding his lost brother or sister.

In an article in *Twins Magazine* Sheryl McInnis observed that "Parents must be very careful about how they discuss death. If it is glorified, or if the child is told that when he dies he will join his twin, they may be laying the groundwork for an attempted suicide. One mother noted that for a few months after his twin died, her son did everything he could to put himself in danger. When she drew his attention to what the consequences might be if he were not more careful, he would reply that it didn't matter because if he died he'd be with his brother and have someone to play with again."

According to McInnis, a young child may also

display some personality changes such as becoming destructive or withdrawn. Death is understood better, she noted, by the child as he matures and learns to put time in perspective and to develop his own sense of mortality. However, even children in their teens need to talk about their feelings. They may be experiencing the guilt of survival and now having a greater share of the parents' attention.

McInnis points out that "The twin who has a solid sense of his separate self will feel the loss as profoundly as one who does not, but the more mature twin may be able to work through the grieving process with less lasting pain than the twin with little or no separate identity."

CLIMB, Center for Loss in Multiple Birth, is an incorporated group organized in Alaska. CLIMB's purpose is to give support to parents who have experienced the death of one, both or all of their children during a twin or higher multiple pregnancy, at birth, or in infancy. This organization has a quarterly publication called *Our Newsletter,* which is listed in the back under Resources.

8

Prenatal Loss

RECENTLY A VERY TOUCHING STORY of a mother and daughter was shared with me. Sarah Smith had lived with the feeling that there was something missing all her life, even before she was told at fourteen that she had survived her twin even before birth. Her mother had five children in seven years. Ten years later she became pregnant. She had an abortion in her fourth month of pregnancy and six weeks later felt a kicking in her abdomen. Her doctor told her that she had been carrying twins and somehow one had been aborted and one had survived and was growing. He and several other doctors urged her to have a second abortion, claiming that if the baby survived it would be brain damaged. Sarah's mother decided to keep the baby. Sarah, now 22, is a pre-med student with outstanding grades.

Sarah writes, "It is excruciatingly painful to me to deal with the reality of being a twin and feeling the bonding that took place and feeling like he's here, and needing him so desperately, wanting him, and yet to know I will never have him. Never to know what he looks like, can he sing also like I can? Would he also have been interested in the medical field? The worst part of all is to know that I'm here alive today at the expense of his life. The feelings that go through me are so confusing. One moment, I can feel devastatingly lonely, and not be able to wait for the day when I can die to go meet him in heaven. Just to hug him and tell him how much I love him. Yet at the same time I can feel so incredibly guilty for being alive, like I don't deserve it, so I try to make up for it by being so driven and aggressive with school and work, thinking I don't have a minute to waste, in a sense, to be good enough for two people to make up for me being here and him not."

"I think all twins would agree that being a twin is one of the greatest gifts that God could have given us, and I would encourage twins who have their twin and those that have lost them, to treasure the times you had together. To remember the love, laughter, understanding, bonding, and everything associated with being a twin and to hold on to those memories in light of the fact that even if your twin is gone, you will always be a twin. I thank God and my brother for the gift of life that I have been given, but I long for the day to be with him again. I know that until that day, my soul will be tied to his and no one could ever compare or substitute for my twin."

Glenda French-Welton is a woman whose identical twin died as an infant . She was haunted as an adult by a sense of loss that defied explanation. She describes her experience coming to terms with grief after thirty years.

"I was born one of identical twin girls in 1946. At three months, we developed pneumonia and within hours my twin died. I had no conscious memory of Linda. My parents never tried to deny her. It was a given in my family that there were five children and one had died. I thank my parents for keeping her memory alive.

"When I was about 32, I was struggling with an impending loss and I began to experience grief which seemed all out of proportion to the current situation. I was in therapy at the time. During one particularly memorable session I accessed very early feelings and had a conscious connection to my grief. I was embarrassed to tell my therapist but I was crying so hard it seemed to deserve an explanation so I went ahead. 'I miss my twin. But she died when we were only three months old. How could I possibly miss someone I never knew? Am I crazy?' I sobbed.

"The tears were so cathartic and so primitive that my therapist came to the couch and held me while I cried, and told me I was not crazy. I was able to accept the grief as real and was in mourning for the next few months. I shared this with a few close family members and friends who could understand me.

"This grieving explained two important aspects of my life. One was that I was trying to live a life full enough for two people. When I accepted that, I knew it was not good for me, my family, or for Linda. Yes, for Linda. I felt her spirit powerfully wanting to be free. I had to release her for both our sakes. There developed a significant change in my life when I assumed responsibility for only my life, not both our lives.

"The second thing changed but never ended entirely. Often in a group such as family or at a staff meeting, I get an overwhelmingly real sense that one person is missing and I find myself counting to see who it is. I'm always certain I am missing someone. I used to try to figure out who was missing. Though I have become aware of my longing for my sister, I occasionally have the same experience but now I just understand it is her that I miss."

Elizabeth Noble, in her book *Having Twins,* relates her experience having shared life in utero with a twin. After exploring her prenatal experience under the guidance of Graham Farrant and others she has concluded that her interest in twins stems from her own personal experiences of intra-uterine loss. Noble states that she has made many other connections with the loss of her twin, "including feelings of being wrong, especially the wrong gender, which burdened me for years and led me to seek opposites in my relationships. Running a kindergarten for two sets of twins in my neighborhood when I was a pre-teen, and writing *Having Twins.*"

With permission I share a refreshing experience by one participant in Elizabeth Noble's workshop. "I expected this to be another experiential process I would doze through. But midway through it, when we were those balls of cells fumbling slowly through the tube,I was *there* now. Feeling caressed by the tube, softly following towards something...a very secure feeling. Protected, safe, whole. But my serenity was to be short-lived. As soon as we entered the womb I split and became two. Shortly thereafter (it could have been weeks, the process was timeless), my "other" went away, forever. The vision that I have that goes with it is of a woman riding off into the darkness with her back to me, and all I see is the back wheel of a yellow bicycle, a sort of golden-yellow star rolling away into the darkess. From then on, my entire being, body and all, was bathed in sorrow–a deep all-encompassing despair that permeated the whole universe for me. That was *all*, that was life. It was so *physical*. I was weakened by it."[1]

[1]Excerpt from *Having Twins* by Elizabeth Noble. Copyright © 1980 by Elizabeth Noble. Reprinted by permission of Houghton Mifflin. All rights reserved.

9

Helping One Another

TWINS WHO HAVE EXPERIENCED the loss of
a twin can offer invaluable support to a newly
bereaved twin. It was put in perspective by
Marion Hearn when he wrote to me about the loss of his
identical twin brother, Melvin. Following is an excerpt
from his letter:

"Some of the things I miss are not having Melvin's
helping hand and his part in making decisions. Another
is not being able to pick up the phone and call him or
have him call me on our FM radio system. A vacant
chair in the family circle on many occasions, especially
during the holidays of Thanksgiving, Christmas, and
New Year's, causes a feeling of emptiness.

"From time to time I have to tell myself that Melvin
would be proud of me for what I have done or am doing.
I realize now that when we lost other loved ones we had
the support of each other. One thing our minister told me
I will always remember is 'Hang onto your faith', and
I'd pass that on to anyone else.

"My faith in God, the strength in prayer and the
power of positive thinking, the support of my wife,

family and friends in the community, are all a great support to me. I would suggest to anyone experiencing such a loss that at any time you feel like crying do so. Tears are words of love spoken from the bottom of our hearts. Many times when I realize that I'm a little depressed I switch to the power of positive thinking and think how fortunate I was in being born a twin."

The adjustment to the death of his twin was eloquently described by James S. Wilson in a letter to me. Jim's words are reprinted here with his permission. His message is one that will help relieve the grief of everyone who loses a twin.

"We were born in 1951 and Bill died in 1985. Quite simply stated, this was by far the most devastating event in my life and will always be with the exception of my own death. No one understands the size of the loss. I quit talking about it to people long ago because they don't know how to relate to the loss of one so close.

"Bill and I lived apart for most of our adult lives. He was single and I am in my second, and successful, marriage. We spoke on the phone several times a week and stayed in communication even if one or both of us were out of the country. We tried to visit each other three or more times a year.

"My first wife was extremely jealous of our relationship but Nancy loved him like a brother. She did not pit us against one another like Jane did. To give you an idea of how close we were, I remember the day before he died he realized that he should eat something to maintain strength but could not think of anything that sounded good. Several visitors made suggestions but nothing worked. I took one look at him and said 'ice cream' and he immediately perked up and told us that was the only thing.

"About a week before his death, he was visiting us in Oklahoma City and we decided to go to a Tina Turner concert. I took my camera to get pictures but got caught with it at the gate. They did not allow photographic equipment inside the hall. I left to go back to the car while Nancy and Bill went inside to get seated. Nancy wondered why I was taking so long to return and Bill told her that I was trying to find a way to smuggle the camera past the gate. She disagreed with him saying that I would never do that. About five minutes later in I walked with a sweater over the camera. Nancy was amazed that someone else knew me better than she.

"I won't go into much detail of the events surrounding Bill's death. He'd been sick off and on for years. When I learned of his final illness, we flew to see him not expecting him to die. The shock, no, terror, of seeing him lifeless on that hospital bed burned an unforgettable memory onto my brain. I was not prepared for the magnitude of this event.

"We went about the task of funeral arrangements in one city and then shipping him to our hometown for another service and burial. Calling my parents that day was extremely difficult. I must have been on automatic pilot. The feeling was one of periods of numbness separated by stretches of reality with immense sorrow. I cried so much those days that I developed an ear infection that I still have today.

"Several things I believe helped me get through the grieving. Arranging for the funeral and seeing him dead helped put a finality to his life. Speaking at his service in my hometown was very hard but helped me see the good of his life and recognize the end of it. I spoke because no one else had known him like I did. I'm sure he would have appreciated the fact that I read a Catholic prayer

(St. Francis of Asisi) in a Southern Baptist church. I
talked of his love for life and the great things he did to
help those in need around him. Few knew the vast
amount of time he gave to others with no expectation of
anything in return.

"Since Bill was single, Nancy and I cleaned out his
apartment. We went through everything, bills,
keepsakes, closets, drawers, etc. We would find pictures
and other reminders and laugh and cry. We sold what we
could and took the rest home. It was a very grueling
process but also a healing one.

"Even as I write this letter to you, I find a measure
of relief, which leads me to the most beneficial action I
took, and that is to expressing myself verbally or in
writing to a third party that really cares! At first Nancy
was a tremendous help and so were my older brother and
parents. But there was something big missing and
feelings still were not addressed.

"I went to an expensive psychologist and he helped
some but I could tell that his interest was more at the
financial level than at the soul. I could not seem to get
the knack of going into the session calm and collected,
express myself to a high level of emotion, and then fall
back to 'normal' in a fixed period of time, usually 45
minutes.

"A few months after his death, I contacted the twin
research team at Minnesota University. By chance I
noticed an article in a magazine about the program in
Minnesota. It talked briefly about their study of twin loss
and I called to offer my help. My motivation was to offer
my assistance but I was also looking for a way to fill the
need I had—the need to understand what had happened
to me.

"Dr. Nancy Segal returned my call and we had a

good talk. I later filled out a survey on twin loss that she had sent. A few months later I met her in Oklahoma City at the annual twins convention. Dr. Brandt and others had founded a twin loss support group and this was to be the first meeting. The group met but I found the meeting very inadequate other than it was comforting to know that others had experienced my same loss. The group was named 'Twinless Twins' after my suggestion.

"I found the meeting lacking in that everyone had so many unexpressed feelings and emotions that a one hour meeting each year was like a drop in the ocean. It was clear to me that all of us required one-on-one sessions with a professional or with one of the other members of the group.

"Nancy Segal and I met for over an hour after the meeting and I came away from that talk a different person. She had so many good things to say as well as knew how to listen. I believed her when she said that some questions had no answers. Her combined experience as a twin, trained psychologist, and twin expert, along with a genuine caring helped that missing feeling go away. In the five years after his death it has not returned.

"About two years later I was fortunate to help my old boss with a similar situation. Jerry's identical twin brother was terminally ill with death expected at any moment. Throughout the ordeal family and friends gathered. On several occasions he would come to me to talk because I knew what he was experiencing. I was a friend of them both and it was obvious to me the deep level of their relationship. I still grieved the loss of my brother but I was happy that my experience could help in a way that no one else could offer. For that I am very grateful.

"To me, facing the reality of the loss is the only way to deal with the loss. Eulogizing in my mind keeps the good memories fresh. Although that imprint in my head has never diminished, it does not come back as often. I still have times when it hits me. I break down and cry, mostly by myself, and then I am all right. There are times when something will occur and I will instinctively reach for the phone to call him as I so often did. I have thought of him every day since his death. I dream of him at least once a week (my dreams are another subject entirely which could take another three pages).

"Nancy my wife, made a collage of photographs taken of Bill and me over the years. I proudly display it in my home. There's no need to pretend he didn't exist and that I am no longer a twin. I am still a twin!! Most people do not have a clue as to what to say or how to react when they find out I lost my twin. There's no reason to expect them to know.

"I suggest the following to help other twins deal with their loss:

- *Participate in the funeral arrangements allowing the reality of death to better set in, minimizing denial. Give a eulogy if at all possible.*

- *Examine your feelings and resist the temptation to stuff them by ignoring they exist. They will surface somehow anyway and this is the best way. Talk and express feelings with someone else who can identify with this special loss. Call a member of the Twinless Twins Support Group. Talking helped me the most.*

- *Help someone else who has lost a close relative.*
  You have experienced the worst loss of all and
  know the depths of theirs. Don't force yourself on
  them but make yourself available.

I will never cease to be amazed at the generosity of these twinless twins who tell me of their experiences in losing their twin to death. They tell me that they find comfort in telling their story, since they believe their sharing will help others.

This is what Bruce Abbott had to say as he shared thoughts after losing his identical twin brother, suddenly, at the age of thirteen. Bruce said, "It's almost beyond words to tell you the pain I felt at my brother's death. I expected my friends to be as conscious of my feelings as my brother was, and that was impossible."

Bruce went on to say that, "In my brother's death, since he couldn't succeed at things, because he died, I may have limited myself subconsciously in some things, although I've been successful in many things since his death. Possibly I dragged my feet at times along the way. Because he was not there to succeed, I shouldn't succeed either."

Bruce continued "My life has been filled with so many counterproductive things–a lot of anguish, a lot of hurt. I haven't been able to concentrate and delve into the feelings of my brother's death. He continued, "It is interesting to think of twins who have no other siblings in the family. They have no way of knowing another existence – in a friendship, in caring for somebody, other than their twin brother or sister, especially an identical twin as I was. I didn't know there was any other way of relating to somebody other than the closeness I had with my twin brother. After his death I went out into a world expecting, when I made friends, for us to be as close as he and I were. Not in a conscious way, but in a subconscious, hereditary body-thinking way." He closed by saying "So many people don't understand the closeness of twins."

I have observed that some twins upon losing their twin expend themselves to the limit, wearing themselves out trying to do the work of two. Others felt that they should not achieve, and limited their own success because their twin is no longer able to achieve.

Sherry Nevius, who lost her twin sister, Shawn, developed some strategies for coping which she says helped her.

A touching tribute to her twin was the drawing of a dove that Sherry had a tattoo artist ink on her skin. It was a symbol of hope and peace for Sherry, and a lasting reminder of her love for Shawn.

The following is Sherry's list of coping strategies which she would like to share with others:

- *Give yourself time to heal. (It took me 18 months to feel like my old self).*

- *Set a goal or goals so that you have something to look forward to. I went on a trip overseas in the summer of 1990. My twin sister died in August of 1988.*

- *The day before my sister's wake I bought a tape— Amy Grant, The Collection. Maybe it would help others to buy themselves small gifts as pick me ups because every little bit helps.*

- *Talk to other twins, because twins understand better than anyone else the special bond that exists among 'twinners.'*

- *Laughter is great medicine. It also helps to heal the hurt. A good book or movie did wonders for me.*

- *Join a grief support group if you want or need others who can help you.*

- *Give yourself as much time as it takes to get back to your daily living pattern.*

- *You can either be your own best friend or your worst foe. Strive to get back into the mainstream of living—your twin would want it that way. But do it in time with your rhythm. Each one of us must move in his own way.*

- *Be patient with others, especially family, because unless they are or were a twin they will never truly understand the bond you had.*

- *Be proud of your 'twinship', once a twin always a twin. It's okay to let others know you still consider yourself a twin.*

- *Keep a journal about your feelings. Writing is great therapy. Express your grief, anger, memories, and in time the acceptance of the loss of your twin. No one has to read your journal.*

- *I worked on a painting as a tribute to Shawn and also for my own personal growth and satisfaction.*

- *I had a chance to join the Twinless Twins Support Group but decided against it because I did not feel that it was healthy for me at the time to keep trying to 'hang on' to my sister and wish her back to her earthly physical existence.*

- *Go to church if it helps. My religious faith helped somewhat and I am grateful for it, but I did question and struggle with it more than I ever had for twelve months or so after my twin sister's death."*

Mikki Burrows lost her beloved identical twin sister, Marge, twelve years ago when she choked on a piece of meat. They and a friend were having dinner together. During the meal Marge went to the bathroom while the others continued to visit. Soon they realized Marge had not returned, so Mikki went to check on Marge. She found her on the bathroom floor, blue. Frantically, Mikki called 911 but it was too late. The sudden loss put Mikki in a state of numbness. Right after the funeral she asked to be taken home since she felt as if she were choking. Mikki said she felt as if nobody understood her grief. She said "I was so completely devastated and I felt as if people were trying to compare their grief to mine and as far as I was concerned there was no comparison. I was in my own little world. I didn't want any of them to comfort me because they didn't understand. I remember the first night after her death, I went to her apartment and touched all her personal things and cried out to God, 'Why?'

"I was so completely devastated by her sudden death that I locked out a lot of my feelings. At the funeral I felt that a part of me was in the casket."

Mikki told me that she stopped drinking two months to the day that she buried her twin. Had she not stopped drinking she would not be alive, as she was very suicidal at that time. This twin says that even now after eleven years she often dreams of Marge and in the dream she is alive. Since Mikki and I live in the same town, we have come to know and love one another. I am happy to say that Mikki has come a long way in recovery. She finds that her most difficult time comes when she has her birthday without her twin to share it. Mikki would like other twins to know that one of the things that really helped her in the first year after Marge's death was gathering up all the pictures and mementos pertaining to their twinship that she could find and putting them in an album.

Many twins advise preparing for the inevitable separation by establishing communication early in life–through open dialogue, resolving feelings of anger, jealousy, resentment, and making peace with your twin.

Can anyone, twin or non-twin prepare for the death of a loved one? Following are some suggestions that I believe might be helpful to lighten the shock:

1. *Recognize that the potential for loss is always present.* If this thought is maintained, it should have a direct bearing on how we treat each other. Regret is always painful. It is very hard to accept, especially when it is too late to do anything about it. "If only" is an unfortunate expression all of us know well. We should take time to express our love while there is life.

2. *Cherish the bond of twinship.* The gift you were born with is a special gift. Don't hesitate to tell your twin of your love. For some people it is hard to say "I love you" but after your loved one is gone and you can recall expressing your love for your twin, you will find great comfort. It's too late after he or she is no longer around.

3. *Build a bank of happy memories through shared*

experiences with your twin. Recalling such happy times after you are alone will give you comfort in knowing the pleasure you brought one another.

    4. *Communicate with your twin.* If you have regrets, or recall how you were unkind to your twin as a child, or even in later years, be willing to say I'm sorry, if you feel in your heart you can do so. Try to resolve old resentments and rivalries that may exist. If issues such as these have kept you from a warm loving relationship with your twin, try to let go of those feelings. The best way to have that happen is to unburden yourself with the guilt you may have for harboring such feelings. You may not be prepared for your twin's reaction. Be prepared for soul-searching that might come from each of you. Tears may flow, but they will be cleansing tears, healing tears—tears that may bring with them release and joy. Be prepared for a warm embrace (it could happen) once sharing had taken place—it could be an unforgettable moment!

    Here are twin loss tips that I have gleaned from my reading and from talking to twinless twins.

- Accept your feelings
- Don't deny the loss
- Allow yourself to feel the pain, cry and grieve
- Don't hold on to the past
- Realize that you will heal
- Seek out support groups
- Grieve in your own way and time, without guilt
- Be kind to yourself
- Keep physically and mentally active
- Don't make drastic changes in your usual pattern of living
- Let others comfort you
- Keep your faith alive
- Recall pleasant memories of your twin

- Remember to maintain good nutrition and health habits
- Keeping a journal may be a comfort to you
- Do something different, take up a new hobby, make new friends
- Enlarge your interests, don't dwell on your own problems

Dr. Jane Greer, a psychotherapist who conducts meetings for twinless twins in Douglaston, New York, shared her observation that many twins want to keep their twin alive in some form. Many tell of dreaming often of their twin. Some of them have said they enjoy driving their twin's car or living in their twin's house.

Dr. Francine Siegal, a psychotherapist in Portland, Oregon and a national guest speaker, has treated fraternal and identical twins in moments of difficulty or in times of transition in their adult lives. She writes "All were reasonably intact educated people but there was a common denominator that I have not seen in other patients. This common denominator was particularly strong in identical twins. I will try to define it because I believe its presence contributes to the terrible abandonment feelings that twinless twins experience.

"To me as a therapist, there is a sense (particularly with close identical twins) that the patient experiences themselves and their twin as one entity. Not a couple, but as one being that is larger than one person but smaller than two. That they perceive their own ego boundary as drawn around *both* of them."

Dr. Siegal believes that the more a twin couple blend their egos, the greater their existential experience of never being alone even when physically separated, the deeper their love and commitment, and therefore the greater their feelings of abandonment at death. "The surviving twin is often unduly depressed/lost because they *expect* to make another 'friend'. They hope, for instance, that their child will become this friend. This hope for twin replacement is unrealistic."

Dr. Siegal has also observed that "for some there is an opposite reaction, a sense of relief, or liberation, after a twin's death.This is not an uncommon reaction after the loss of a parent – particularly of a parent who gave criticism or was judgemental by temperament. It can also be a legitimate feeling after the loss of a twin because being a twin is not all roses.

"We are normally the most ambivalent about the people closest to us. However, in the instance of twins, a fraternal twin may feel more of this ambivalence than an identical because they haven't benefited from the soul pleasing mystical oneness type bonding that identicals can feel.

"Twins need to be allowed to feel this emotional relief guiltlessly, then and only then will they be able to fully grieve and then to move on with their lives."

Dr. Siegal gives this information on coping with loss.

"For identical twins especially, appreciate that the loss of the 'Extension of Self' means that the surviving twin will experience a time of disorientation, emptiness, yearning, and profound grief that goes along with suddenly being cast adrift.

"This new experience of singularity can bring with it the awful feelings of abandonment, loneliness, indecisiveness, and/or uncertainty. These feelings are normal.

"When we step back and look at the situation, we see that the twin, in a state of shock at losing their twin, must simultaneously plunge into their maiden voyage as a person, totally alone, uncertain, and scared, as well as grieve for their loss.

"Build on this realization by holding onto a healthy amount of this special person/relationship without isolating yourself further by trying to keep the other person alive by the sheer will of your preoccupation with and memories of the other person. It is not the surviving twin's responsibility to undo the death by making the deceased twin the center of their total existence and thoughts.

"The wish to re-unite is normal. Establish a view consistent with your religious philosophy that allows for this reunion. For instance the belief that your twin is watching over you, or that after your natural time to die you will be together again in heaven.

"If you feel like half of you is in the casket, it is because half of you is. With time you will become aware of a living part of you that when your twin was alive you ignored, which will now grow and develop. You will become complete. Alone, yes, but reasonably complete.

"Seek out comfort and understanding from the Twinless Twin's Support Group that may be in your area. It is a comfort to feel understood.

"Learn to cry, it will heal you. Sometimes you will cry for yourself, sometimes for your twin.

"No one can understand the loss of a child or the loss of a twin, except someone who has lost one. So don't expect it.

"Believe that with time the pain will lessen and become bearable. One secret to a successful life is flexibility and resiliency. Roll with the punches.

"Another is to recreate family, friends, and community over and over again in your lifetime as you lose those dear to you. Do this be reaching out. Sad to say, the world is too busy to find you.

"Heal by healing others. Grieve by aiding others to grieve. Start with those in your family. Compassion is healing.

"Do not try or expect to replace your twin. That is impossible. But do make new intimate friendships–they will not be as close but they are special and loving. You may already know the person who will become the next special friend. Perhaps you never gave them a chance before.

"Seek solace in your religion through prayer or meditation.

"Try to get the tormented feelings out of your body. Write them down, speak them to friends or to a support group, or seek out a psychotherapist. Do not hold them inside of you or they can become morbid.

"Remember the good things. Collect photos or write down vignettes. There are times when looking through these can be a comfort to you or to their children.

"Believe in yourself. Look within yourself for strength. Pray for it. It is there. All it takes is your believing it.

"Anniversary Reactions are illnesses or depressions that occur yearly around the anniversary of a bad event. The anniversary of your twin's death, your birthday, or perhaps the holidays. If this happens to you, preparing for it is half the battle. You may want to be alone for part of the time. It's also good to plan to be with a loving friend for the rest of the time.

"It's not possible to live for two–if you try you'll just fail at living. You are not expected to make your twin's hopes and dreams come true. If your twin had stayed alive they may have changed their mind anyway.

The best you can do, and probably what your twin really wants for you, is to live honestly and fully as a person in your own right in balance with the needs and goals of *your* family and community."

Resources

The following sources may prove helpful to those who need some encouragement or someone willing to listen and with whom to share:

AMBA (Australian Multiple Birth Assoc., Inc.)
P.O. Box 105
Coogee, NSW 2034, Australia

Association for Pre-Perinatal Health
1600 Prince Street, Suite 500
Alexandria, VA 22314-2838
(703) 548-2802
FAX (703) 548-2808

CLIMB (Center for Loss In Multiple Birth)
Jean Kollantai
P.O. Box 1064
Palmer, AK 99645
(907) 746-6123

The Compassionate Friends, Inc.
P.O. Box 3696
Oak Brook, IL 60522-3696
(312) 990-0010

Dr. Jane Greer, Ph.D.
Twin Consultant
42-46 235th Street
Douglaston, NY 11363
(718) 423-9703

Elizabeth Kubler-Ross Center
South Route 616
Head Waters, VA 24442
(703) 396-3441

Minnesota Twin Loss Project
University of Minnesota
75 E. River Rd.
Minneapolis, MN 55455
(612) 625-3372

Multiple Births Foundation
Institute of Obstetrics and
    Gynecology Trust
Queen Charlottes' and Chelsea Hospital
Goldhawk Road
London, England W6OXG
(01) 748-4666, Ext. 6201

National Organization of Mothers of
    Twins Clubs, Inc.
(NOMOTC), 12402 Princess Jeanne N.E.
Albuquerque, NM 87112-4640
(505) 275-0955

Eileen M. Pearlman, Ph.D.
1137 Second Street, Suite 209
Santa Monica, California 90403
(310) 458-9723

The Premature and High Risk Infant Assoc., Inc.
P.O. Box A-3083
c/o West Glen Branch
Peoria, IL 61614

POMBA of Canada, Inc.
Parents of Multiple Births
   Association of Canada, Inc.
P.O. Box 2300
Lethbridge, Alberta
Canada, T1J4K7
(403) 328-9165

Pregnancy and Infant Loss Center
1415 E. Wayzata Blvd., Suite 22
Wayzata, MN 55391
(612) 473-9372

Darcie D. Sims, Ph.D.
Grief Therapist
P.O. Box 92032
Albuquerque, NM 87199
(505) 275-1690

Nancy L. Segal
California State University, Fullerton
Dept. of Psychology
800 N. State College Boulevard
Fullerton, CA 92634
(714) 773-3514

Francine M. Siegal, M.D.
1809 N.W. Johnson Street
Portland, OR 97209
(503) 221-1046

TAMBA Bereavement Support Group
41 Fortuna Way, Aylesby Park
Grimsby, South Humberside, DN 37951

Tender Hearts
24134 Rimview Rd.
Moreno Valley, CA 92387
(714) 924-2045

Twin Services, Inc.
P.O. Box 10066
Berkeley, CA 94709
(415) 644-0861

Twinless Twins Support Group
Dr. Raymond W. Brandt, Ph.D.
11220 St. Joe Rd.
Fort Wayne, IN 46815
(219) 627-5414

Suggested Reading

Aiken, Lewis R. *Dying, Death and Bereavement.* Allyn. 1991.

Alexander, Victoria G. *Words I Never Thought to Speak: Stories of Life in the Wake of Suicide.* Free Press.1991.

Braunstein, Miriam P. *Understanding Twins.* Sigo Press. 1991.

Cook, Alicia S. and Dworkin, Daniel S. *Helping the Bereaved: Therapeutic Interventions for Children, Adolescents and Adults.* Basic. 1992.

D'Arcy, Paula. *When Your Friend is Grieving: Building a Bridge of Love.* Shaw Publications. 1990.

Doka, Kenneth and Morgan, John D; eds. *Death and Spirituality.* Baywood Publishing. 1990.

Dykstra, Robert. *She Never Said Good-Bye: One Man's Journey Through Grief.* Shaw Publications. 1989.

Fitzgerald, Helen. *The Grieving Child: A Parent's Guide.* S&S Trade. 1992.

Green, Gerald. *Coping with Suicide: A Pastoral Aid.* Columbia Press. 1992.

Grollman, Earl A. *Straight Talk about Death for Teenagers: How to Cope with Losing Someone You Love.* Beacon Press. 1993.

Henley, Linda. *A Time To Mourn...A Time to Dance. A Young Widow's Reflections on God's Will.* Levite Apache. 1990.

Kay, Alan A. *A Jewish Book of Comfort.* Aronson. 1993.

Kubler-Ross, Elizabeth. *On Death and Dying, and On Children and Death.* McMillan.

Kutscher, Austin H.; et al, eds. *For the Bereaved: The Road to Recovery.* Charles. 1990.

Leon, Irving G. *When a Baby Dies: Psychotherapy for Pregnancy and Newborn Loss.* Yale University Press. 1990.

Lightner, Candy and Hathaway, Nancy. *Giving Sorrow Words: How to Cope with Grief and Get on with Your Life.* Warner Books.

Linn, Erin. *Children Are Not Paper Dolls: A Visit With Bereaved Siblings.* Pub Mark. 1982.

Morgan, John D.; ed. *The Dying and Bereaved Teenager.* Charles. 1990.

Noble, Elizabeth. *Inside Experiences: Guided Recall for Birth & Before,* (audiotape). Available from Women's Health Resources, 448 Pleasant Lake Ave., Harwich, MA 02645, (508) 432-8040, FAX 432-9685.

Noble, Elizabeth. *Having Twins: A Parental Guide to Pregnancy, Birth & Early Childhood.* Boston: Houghton Mifflin. 1991.

Noble, Elizabeth. *Primal Connections: How Our Experiences From Conception Through Birth Influence our Emotions, Behavior & Health.* NY: Simon & Schuster. 1993.

Pardoe, Jenifer. *How Many Times Can You Say Good-Bye?* Liturgical PR.

Sims, Darcie D., Ph.D.*Why Are the Casseroles Always Tuna? A Loving Look at the Lighter Side of Grief.* Big A & Company.

Sims, Darcie D., Ph.D.*Footsteps Through the Valley.* Big A & Company. 1993.

Sims, Darcie D., Ph.D.*If I Could Just See Hope.* Big A & Company. 1993.

Smolin, Ann and Guinan, John. *Healing After the Suicide of a Loved One.* Simon & Schuster. 1993.

Visitacion, Elaine. *Lori...Where Are You? A Mother's Experience of Grief and Loss.* 1993.

Bereavement, a Magazine of Hope and Healing
Bereavement Publishing, Inc.
8133 Telegraph Drive
Colorado Springs, Colorado 80920
(719) 282-1948
Fax (719) 282-1850

Index

Epilogue

In this small book you have heard twins speak. Since I am still blessed in having my twin on this earth with me I can only try to understand what these twins are experiencing as they live their life without their twin. Their messages are meant to help not only those who have lost a twin, but those who still have their twin. Losing our twin to death is a thought we prefer to put out of our mind, yet, as Caroline Tancredy taught us in the book, she found great comfort because she and Mary had recognized the inevitability of loss of one or the other and had open discussions on how they would continue to comfort one another even if they were physically separated by death.

Just weeks before this book went to print, Isabel Rogers, an identical twin, called me. Four months ago her twin was seriously injured in a car crash. For weeks her sister seemed to be making a rapid recovery and plans were made to move her home. Just before she was to leave the hospital she took a turn for the worse and died. High hopes were dashed and reality set in. Isabel's twin would not be going home. Isabel's nephew, son of her twin sister, is a scientist and told Isabel "You and my mother were genetically alike and now I have lost my mother. Would you mind if I now consider you mother and could you speak of me as your son?"

When Isabel shared this with me I thought how beautiful and what a comfort and aid in healing this will be for both Isabel and her 'son'. Since I understand the tightly knit bond that exists between twins, I am confident that Isabel's twin sister would feel that this is the highest tribute that can be made to her.

Parents of small twins can do so much to help prepare them for the time when they will lose their twin.

1. Let them see themselves as individuals who were blessed to be born with another their age.

2. Encourage them to be supportive of one another in whatever they choose.

3. Provide them with opportunities to build upon their own strengths independent of their twin.

4. Make it possible for them to build their own network of friends.

5. Teach them to respect one another; not allowing them to mistreat and hurt each other, physically and verbally.

6. Give them a chance to know of a power greater than their own; to have faith that, even if their twin is physically no longer with them, there is promise that they will one day be joined in eternity.

Only you know where you are in your journey through life. Only you, with God's help can make changes in your life that will make the journey lighter.

If you are one who has lost your twin, I pray that you have found help within these pages. For you who still have your twin, I also pray that you do whatever you can now, to ease the loss when one twin is no longer living.

The last thought that I would like to leave you with is: Hold onto your faith.

Order Form

To order *Living Without Your Twin,* enclose check for $9.95. Shipping and handling: $2.00 for the first book and $1.00 for each additional book.

To order *We Are Twins But Who Am I?* (hardcover), enclose check for $18.95. Shipping and handling: $3.00 for the first book and $1.00 for each additional book.

Send postal orders to Tibbutt Publishing, 0438 SW Palatine Hill Road, Portland, OR 97219, USA. 1-800-621-5655.

For credit card orders call toll free: Upper Access (Visa, MasterCard, Discover Card, and American Express) 1-800-356-9315.

Name _____

Address_____

City _____

State _____

Zip _____

Telephone_____